Leisure and the Environment

John Spink

Butterworth-Heinemann Ltd
Linacre House, Jordan Hill, Oxford OX2 8DP
ℛ A member of the Reed Elsevier plc group

OXFORD   LONDON   BOSTON
MUNICH   NEW DELHI   SINGAPORE   SYDNEY
TOKYO   TORONTO   WELLINGTON

First published 1994
Reprinted 1995

British Library Cataloguing in Publication Data
Spink, John
    Leisure and the Environment   3Rev.ed
    I. Title
    306.4

ISBN 0 7506 0687 8

Printed and bound in Great Britain by
Biddles Ltd, Guildford and King's Lynn

Contents

Preface

This text has developed from my personal interest and teaching in leisure, social policy and urban studies. Its production, however, is entirely due to the encouragement and support of a number of professional colleagues. Teaching on the Ilkley Campus of Bradford and Ilkley Community College in the late 1980s brought me into contact with the then leisure 'team' of Les Haywood, Frank Kew, Ian Henry, Peter Bramham, John Capenerhurst, and Pete Livesey. They have all given enormous support and encouragement in teaching and research. A particular debt, however, is owed to Ian Henry and Peter Bramham with whom I have shared enjoyable and fruitful research on the city of Leeds, and even more enjoyable social events which have welded professional interests with lasting friendship.

A further debt of gratitude is also owed to Les Haywood as series editor for Butterworth-Heinemann for his patience and long-suffering forbearance, without whom, it is true to say, none of this would have been written. Last, but not least, I wish to record my thanks to my family for their support and help in that Katy Spink typed a substantial section of the text, while Emily and Lucy endured lengthy commentaries whenever we ventured into the countryside. Needless to say, any shortcomings in the volume are entirely my own responsibility.

John Spink

Introduction

Pleasurable free time depends in great part on having a pleasant context within which leisure activities can take place. Accordingly the leisure environment is of great significance in determining the degree of satisfaction derived from any activity. An attractive environment enhances any leisure time for the participant and so this book takes as its central focus that context. Pleasant or unpleasant, the location and context of activity are intrinsic parts of the experience and so the analysis of the leisure environment is an important aspect of any study of leisure.

Leisure environments generate as many issues and problems as does leisure itself. The diversity of human behaviour contained in people's free time ensures that a multiplicity of locations, facilities, situations and environments come into play. Everything from undeveloped beach lines, uplands and woodlands, to the most mechanized theme-park attractions fall within the remit of this text as it attempts to deepen understanding of the implications of environment for leisure and, conversely, the impact of leisure on our environment.

Leisure environments can be divided broadly in terms of individuals' activity spaces between the frequently visited, well known and intimately and continually encountered domain, like the area of home or neighbourhood, and the distant, remote and less known locations visited infrequently. This dichotomy, between the intimate domain, which is commonplace and everyday, and the distant domain, which is special and exciting, corresponds to people's knowledge of the world. On a temporal basis we have most experience of the local area where we live, shop, go to school, play most often, and a diminishing direct knowledge of places beyond that realm (see Figure I.1).

Our knowledge expands according to our age and our mobility, whether or not we are car-owners for instance, so that we gradually build a picture of the outside world as a place of leisure-time pursuits. Childhood is usually prescribed and constrained, but with maturity and increasing mobility our access to a wider action space develops commensurately. Places we occupy most frequently have long-term implications for our leisure lifestyles. They constrain and may even determine our opportunities for leisure

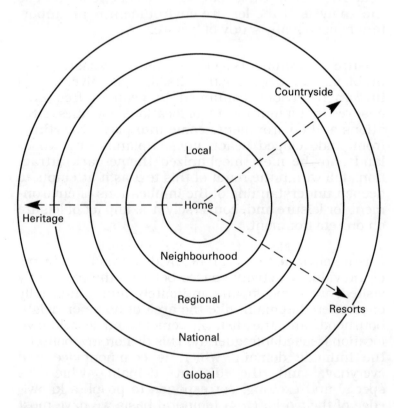

Figure I.1 Leisure action spaces

through education, job vacancies, income, peer groupings, social settings, housing quality, and every other aspect of our life chances. For most of us these local environments are likely to be the city or suburban streets we grow up in or occupy in later life.

Beyond this area of home and neighbourhood lies a wider world, experienced weekly, monthly, annually or even 'once in a lifetime'. Our relation to this outside world is necessarily more tangential and may be quite infrequent or distant. We view it not as 'locals' but much more as tourists, gaining satisfaction from its very difference from home and neighbourhood and maybe even its exoticism. This outside world, at regional, national and global scale, presents a different set of opportunities and facilities from our home-based action space, and this may be, in large part, its very attractiveness to us.

Whether we travel there to enjoy the countryside in rural retreat to a non-urban landscape, or to see historic sites and monuments forming a national or global heritage, or simply visit recognized tourist resorts for holidaymaking, we make particular efforts in travelling further than usual. We leave our commonplace realm and enter another as a day tripper, a holidaymaker or a tourist. Each role links environment and activity in a way that this text will explore further as it investigates the diversity of leisure activities.

In an examination of the relation between leisure and environment, one feature this text seeks to address, if not to redress, is the balance of attention given to urban areas. Most of us live all our lives in urban areas and certainly spend the vast proportion of our free time there. Over 80 per cent of the British population are urban dwellers, so it is the urban environment that dominates the concerns of this text.

Although rural areas are important for contrasting breaks, holidays and day trips, such 'outings' are not

the everyday experience of citizens in towns and suburbs. It is the great cities and conurbations that form
the environment for the majority of people's free time
and come to dominate the leisure of the rest of the
population. You get some idea of the dominance of
metropolitan culture whenever an inch of snow falls
on Central London. Whatever the state of the weather
in the rest of the country, the London-based media
quickly inform us of the 'cataclysm' and its every
impact. However remote one's location, the media
present a city-centred view of existence and come to
influence leisure-time experience to a greater or lesser
extent for all of us.

It is this urban-dominated leisure that forms the
focus of this text. While many approaches to 'environment' emphasize rural and countryside recreation,
the significance of the latter needs to be kept in proportion. For most people the approved middle-class
muscular bias of fell walking, rambling, naturalism
and landscape appreciation forms little part of their
free time activity. Less 'morally uplifting' pursuits like
television and video-viewing, smoking, drinking, gam-
bling, sex, reading popular fiction, playing computer
games, eating out, or simply hanging around shopping centres, form more usual leisure pursuits, while
the more active at least venture out for gardening,
dog-walking and fishing, in often less than sylvan settings.

The leisure pursuits of an urbanized population merit
the attention of all students of leisure. With more free
time available for many members of society and more
resources devoted to leisure spending, the growth of
urban and rural leisure has been a significant feature
of recent social change. This text examines the environmental influences and consequences of such
changes.

The diversity of leisure spaces and places partly
accounts for the interdisciplinary approach adopted

by this study. Environments so different as open moorland or prefabricated sports halls demand a range of differing approaches. For some an ecological dimension is clearly relevant, whereas for others the built environment may demand understanding of political intervention and the rationale behind state or local subsidy. No one approach can cope with the variety of settings enjoyed in contemporary leisure, so an interdisciplinary or multidisciplinary approach broadly founded in the social sciences seems essential for investigating this broadly based feature of human behaviour. Making sense of leisure behaviour is therefore concerned with aspects of economics in the running of facilities or the subsidizing of landscapes; aspects of sociology in the nature and selection of participants, their values and objectives; aspects of politics in the organization and ordering of locations and facilities; and aspects of geography in the analysis of the nature and location of leisure resources and their implications.

This book will combine aspects of all these disciplines in an attempt to make understanding leisure environments accessible to a wide range of students and interests. The breadth of approach seems essential to encompass the diversity of opportunities, and conflicts, that exist. Issues of power, people, and place are crucial to the enjoyment of leisure time. An approach to their understanding demands a disciplinary flexibility commensurate with the diversity of activities encountered.

Questions and exercises

1 Where were your play spaces as a child? Which environments were most significant for your leisure-time activities and which skills or abilities did you develop in which places ?
2 Think about the holiday resorts you have visited since childhood. Do they fit a growing pattern of

knowledge of the world, becoming increasingly more distant from home as you grow older?
3 Construct a spatial and temporal 'map' of your own leisure times and places. What facilities are visited on a daily or weekly basis, and which places on a monthly, annual or 'one off' trip basis? How large is your leisure action space?
4 How do leisure spaces change with increasing age?
5 How much of your leisure time is urban based or affected by urban influences?

Leisure environments in the 1990s

1

Contemporary leisure

The location of leisure in the 1990s has been influenced by two countervailing factors. One reflects the fact that over two-thirds of British households are owner-occupiers. Consequently, rising standards of housing amenity have increased the focus on the home as the location of increasingly individualized and privatized consumption of leisure-time activities. The other, and somewhat contradictory, influence is that over two-thirds of households, often the same prosperous home-owners, now have access to one or more private cars. This permits them great mobility and gives access to a wide variety of local and distant facilities. These two divergent facets, one localized and the other dispersed, have generated a complex pattern of leisure participation and expenditure that shows every sign of continuing into the next century.

Homes foster an inward-oriented, usually individualized leisure activity, exerting a basically centripetal force on leisure distributions, given the urban location of 90 per cent of UK housing. Cars encourage a more centrifugal leisure momentum, since mobility enables and encourages a widening leisure use of a range of more distant opportunities, both urban and rural. Each of these contradictory trends is represented in the data on contemporary leisure patterns.

With almost total penetration of homes, since 98 per cent of households own a television, it is perhaps not surprising that watching TV continues to dominate domestic free time (an average of nearly 27 hours per person per week in 1992, according to *Social Trends*, 1994). The large number of homes equipped with video recorders, satellite receivers, CD players, personal computers and games machines, encourages domestic leisure. Add to these distractions the growth of gardening and do-it-yourself activities, and it is easy to see why so much free time is spent around home-base.

Outdoor leisure away from home is closely linked to income and car ownership. Professional and managerial groups are much more likely to engage in walking, jogging, cycling and sports than semi-skilled and unskilled workers.

Use of cars has encouraged recreational trips for sightseeing and leisure shopping among almost all groups in the population. Like home ownership, however, despite the broad national figures of increased car use (see Table 1.1), there remain localized differences reflecting social polarization and pockets of disadvantage. While areas in the outer South East of England like Surrey Heath and Hart have over 50 per cent of households with access to two or more cars, inner urban areas like Glasgow City, Hackney and Tower Hamlets had over 60 per cent of households without car access in 1991.

Table 1.1 Car access by households (%) 1990

	No car	One car	Two or more cars
England	32	44	23
Wales	30	49	21
Scotland	42	41	17
Northern Ireland	34	47	19
Great Britain	33	44	23

Source: *Social Trends*, 1993

Spending on leisure now accounts for over 16 per cent of household expenditure and is linked to the patterns described earlier. Car-borne mobility has encouraged day tourism and the growth of holiday spending to encompass more than one family vacation for over 25 per cent of households every year. After holidays, alcoholic drink and meals consumed away from home take another substantial slice of total spending (see Table 1.2).

This pattern of consumption matches that which might be expected for an affluent and increasingly car-using population, although the drinking element has traditionally been associated with younger males. Home-based pursuits are also represented in spending on audio and electrical entertainments, on newspapers and periodicals and on materials for gardening and do-it-yourself activities. Traditional forms of spending, whether on cinema, despite the popularity of the multi-screens, theatre, or sports spectating, play a much-diminished role alongside those complementing lifestyles based around car and home.

The gradual changes in leisure spending have reflected changes not only in public tastes and aspirations, as an increasingly affluent population has come to expect more free time and more from its free time, but also a changing population structure. Households have continued to decrease in size so that over one third are two person, while over a quarter are one person. Fewer children have made traditional concepts like the 'family household' relevant for less than a quarter of households. More households are headed by lone parents, particularly mothers, and there are many more independent elderly. An ageing population structure has added to the focus on the home as a location of free time with over 20 per cent of the population over 60 years of age.

As with all household groups, the elderly may be restricted to home-based leisure through limited

Table 1.2 UK household expenditure on selected leisure items

	Pounds per week at 1992 prices		
	1986	1991	1992
Alcoholic drink consumed away from home	8.40	7.85	7.79
Meals consumed out (eaten on the premises but excluding school and workplace meals)	6.19	6.24	6.10
Books, newspapers, magazines etc.	3.86	3.80	3.84
TV, video and audio equipment purchases	4.14	4.77	5.20
Rentals, including licence fees	2.81	2.31	2.39
Home computers	0.23	0.54	0.61
Purchase of materials for home repairs, etc	4.33	4.07	3.96
Holidays	7.61	10.21	11.21
Hobbies	0.09	0.13	0.07
Cinema admissions	0.14	0.19	0.19
Theatre, concert, etc. admissions	0.41	0.53	0.55
Subscription and admission charges to participant sports	1.01	1.10	1.50
Spectator sport admissions	0.16	0.19	0.24
Sports goods (not clothes)	0.52	0.45	0.52
Other entertainment	0.70	0.84	0.88
Total weekly expenditure on above	£40.60	£43.22	£45.05
Expenditure on above items as % of total household expenditure	16.1	16.1	16.6

Source: *Social Trends*, 1994

income. Part of the attraction of TV and radio is its relative cheapness as well as its easy availability. Income remains a crucial determinant of leisure location, whether in the attractions of a large, well equipped home and garden, or in the limitations imposed through reliance on public transport. The divisions in free time between home-base and more distant facilities are as unequal and divisive as all other facets of society, whether determined by fashion, taste, income or opportunity, and are central in determining the pattern of current leisure-time activity.

Leisure lifestyles

Access to leisure facilities and opportunities is determined by a number of factors – availability, investment, suitability, mobility, awareness, etc. – but for most people the critical influence is that of income. Particular groups in society are likely to find their access restricted by money. Groups like the elderly, women, racial minorities, the unemployed and the disabled may well be limited in the amount of spending they can devote to recreational activities. The social reality of poverty tends to act in a mutually reinforcing way, so that those on a limited income are also likely to live in a poorly equipped home environment, often at high density, and to lack access to private transport. The multiple disadvantages of living in the inner city or on a sprawling peripheral housing estate severely inhibit the life chances and leisure opportunities of inhabitants.

Whether this disadvantage is analysed in terms of Marxist sociology through class and life chances, or through Weberian sociology as status and lifestyle, the reality is a relatively deprived experience of leisure activities. Low incomes mean that a larger proportion must be spent on necessities like housing, heating costs and food bills, with a restricted amount available for pleasure (Table 1.3).

For all such groups in society there are a number of similar issues affecting their access to leisure. Groups in poverty lack 'effective demand' in economic terms in that they have limited spending power and so do not attract investment in facilities aimed for their use. They are usually seen as marginal users of facilities, to be only partially catered for and then often as a 'concession'. Social factors, too, tend to work against these groups, in that their image is usually a negative one, which restricts individuals' own access and self-regard under the restrictions of society's disapproving gaze.

Table 1.3 Household spending in the UK, by percentage

	1971	1981	1986	1990	1991	1992
Food	20.1	16.4	13.8	12.3	12.3	12.1
Clothing and footwear	8.5	6.7	7.0	6.1	5.9	5.7
Housing	12.4	14.9	15.3	14.2	14.6	15.4
Fuel and power	4.5	5.1	4.6	3.6	4.0	3.8
Household goods and services	7.8	6.9	6.7	6.5	6.5	6.5
Transport and communication	14.3	17.2	17.5	18.3	17.3	17.2
Alcoholic drink	7.3	7.3	6.9	6.4	6.6	6.6
Tobacco	4.8	3.6	3.1	2.5	2.7	2.7
Recreation, entertainment and education	8.8	9.4	9.4	10.0	10.0	10.0
Other goods, services and adjustments	11.4	12.5	15.6	20.0	20.0	20.0

Source: *Social Trends*, 1994

Politically, such groups are seen as marginal to the main national and local electorates and as such are under-represented in decision-making forums. Any provision made by bureaucratic decision-makers may well correspond to their own stereotypical notion of what racial minorities, women's or elderly groups 'want' or 'like' and hence the organization of discos, badminton and whist drives may well proceed without any expectation of substitutability of choice or participation. Accordingly, each group experiences its own socio-cultural limitations on access to the wider leisure environment (see Table 1.4).

Although for academic convenience it is helpful to consider people in these broad categories it is crucial to remember that each person experiences their leisure opportunities and constraints as an individual, and thus not let the utility of such aggregations or stereotypes mask the essential individuality involved. Grouping may provide useful generalization but it cannot substitute for consideration of each person's unique circumstances.

Table 1.4 Discriminatory factors in leisure provision -

	Economic factors	*Social factors*	*Political factors*
Women	Low pay Caring/dual role Reserve labour force	Constrained action-space Sexism Limited car access Social roles	Male decision- makers Patriarchy Limited provision Sexist stereotypes
Racial minorities	Low pay Reserve labour force	Constrained action-space Racism Closure	White decision- makers Colonialist racist stereotypes
Elderly	Welfare dependence Pension Poverty	Fear Immobility Image	Marginalized Limited provision Ageist stereotypes
Unemployed	Welfare Benefit dependence Poverty	Limited mobility Marginalized Image Work-centred society	Social order provision Concessions
Disabled	Low pay or benefit dependence	Limited mobility Access Image	Ableist decisions Lack of awareness or consultation

Women

For many women the restrictions of economic disadvantage or dependence on a partner's income are particularly telling. Traditionally the majority of women
have worked in the home or in low-paid jobs, often in
a part-time or temporary capacity, with career progression restricted through sexism or interrupted by
child-rearing. Low pay and insecurity have tended to
limit the economic capital and income available, particularly for working class women, who have been
forced, in many cases, to restrict their own leisure
spending and free time in order to secure household
necessities like food and housing costs. Even with
growing affluence and career opportunities for some,
the time constraints of dual employment and domestic roles have limited available leisure opportunities
and increased the physical and mental demands on
individual women.

Perhaps just as important as the economic constraints have been the socio-cultural restrictions that
have limited women's 'action-space' – the environment over which individuals range on a daily or regular basis. For women the social restrictions of image
and role are significant in limiting the facilities and
opportunities available in leisure time. Women as a
group and individually are particularly subject to
societal conceptions of 'acceptability' in behaviour,
both spatially and temporally. Their leisure action-
space is limited to suitable places and suitable times.
To venture outside socially approved realms is to be
'asking for trouble', whether this is in the public bar
or the betting shop, to be alone in parts of the city
centre at night, or even out on moorland as a
solitary walker.

Contrast these with 'appropriate' settings, whether
Women's Institute meetings, further education
courses at night school, step aerobics, bingo as a particular refuge of working-class women, or 'hen' nights,

when there seems little threat to women, or perhaps more importantly, their menfolk's power over their lives. The restrictions on leisure action-space are real, for they are internalized and reinforced through people's fears, real or imaginary, and they have served to restrict and modify women's behaviour considerably. Even the increased domestic focus of leisure may particularly disadvantage women if the presence of male household members merely serves to increase 'her' chores in order to service *their* leisure.

Think of the differences in action-space between men and women of similar ages. There are many places where men would be free to go where women would feel, or be made to feel, 'out of place'. Considerations of seasonality, through hours of darkness, even in urban settings, continue to act as a constraint. Fear of social harassment, or, more frighteningly, physical attack, is a potent restriction on the leisure freedom of individual women and plays a large part in restricting still further their gendered leisure environment.

Additionally, women also have to combat a man-made environment. The majority of decision-makers, whether councillors, architects, planners or developers are still resolutely male. This patriarchal arrangement ensures that the urban and rural built environment makes scant provision for bus users, pushchair access, childcare facilities, the 90 per cent of single parent households, or women needing to combine paid work with domestic roles. The large and small implications of a multiplicity of decisions can affect women's access to leisure, and the political realm is just as unequal as the economic and the social (Little, Peake and Richardson,1988).

The interaction of these three major factors combines to give women a particularly constrained leisure environment. This restricted free time action-space may be limited still further by the additional constraints of race, age, or disability.

Racial minorities

The leisure environment of racial minority individuals and households is equally subject to a range of constraints. As low-paid and often insecure labour, many black people share with women an unequal role in the labour market. Historically, skills and qualifications obtained overseas have not been recognized and the concentration of black workers in unskilled and semi-skilled occupations has ensured that their average earning power is less than that of white workers.

Most of the disadvantages in the labour market are no longer the result of being 'migrants', however, but reflect the interaction of structural changes in demand, poor schooling and low levels of training, disruptive inner urban peer pressures and poverty, and above all, informal and institutionalized racism. The impact is particularly apparent for the prospects of some groups of young people (see Table 1.5).

Table 1.5 Economic activity rates by age, sex and ethnic group, Spring 1993 (Great Britain)

| | | | | | | Per centages | |
						Males	Females
	16–19	20–29	30–39	40–49	50–59/64	16–64	16–59
White	62.0	82.1	84.5	86.7	69.0	86.1	71.9
Black	41.7	75.2	75.2	87.3	70.3	80.4	66.0
Indian	25.1	72.5	77.6	86.3	61.3	80.8	61.4
Pakistani/ Bangladeshi	35.4	52.8	52.1	50.2	41.1	72.3	24.8

Source: *Social Trends*, 1994

Low pay and widespread poverty has formed a real constraint for many households of Afro-Caribbean and Asian origin, and has for the majority ensured a concentration in the run-down and deteriorating housing of inner cities. While ethnic minority groups formed over 6 per cent of the English population in the 1991 Census, they represented less than 1 per cent of the rural population but over 20 per cent of the population of Greater London, including over a third of the population of such inner boroughs as Brent, Newham, Tower Hamlets and Hackney. Other concentrations occurred in inner urban areas of Leicester, the West Midlands and the Northern conurbations.

Discrimination in job opportunities has reflected wider social factors based on the post-colonial ideology of racism. The leisure action-space of racial minorities has been restricted in ways that parallel the limits placed upon women. Racism has led to the exclusion of racial minorities from leisure facilities both overtly and covertly. Using a process of 'social closure', white groups have colluded to ensure that racial minorities are excluded either through being made to feel unwelcome or 'out of place', or in extreme cases through threats and physical violence. These pressures, both subtle and explicit, have worked to perpetuate segregation in many aspects of leisure-time activity when people naturally take the easy way and do not 'look for trouble'.

In consequence, there have developed a range of parallel social, sports and recreational facilities, even churches, serving racial minority communities. Some have derived from racist opposition to racial minority participation in wider society, while others have grown in response to ethnic concerns for shared cultural symbolism, which has led to the creation of community facilities. The two elements of external racism and internal ethnicity are difficult to separate but they interact to perpetuate segregated life-styles and leisure activities.

In few cases has political intervention worked to diminish the separation and isolation. In most instances the concern has been with social order in areas like the inner city, and leisure policy has frequently been an adjunct of more direct forms of policing black behaviour. The stereotypical provision often reflects a lack of knowledge by white decision-makers as well as a limited allocation of resources. Both combine to perpetuate the limitations on racial minority leisure environments, particularly in inner urban settings.

Elderly

For people growing older the difficulties posed by physical deterioration are often exacerbated by a reduction in economic circumstance. For once relatively affluent wage-earners, dependence on a pension may well come to curtail leisure opportunities for those in the lower socio-economic groups. Limited assets and shrinking capital inhibit activity just as much as declining mobility and increasing frailty. Indeed, with increasing life expectancy (see Table 1.6), the stereotypes of the elderly need to be continually revised as a greater proportion of citizens continue to enjoy active independence for longer.

Table 1.6 Life expectancy at birth, UK, 1901–2001

	1901	1931	1961	1981	1991	2001
Males	45.5	58.4	67.9	70.8	73.2	74.5
Females	49.0	62.4	73.8	76.8	78.8	79.9

Source: *Social Trends*, 1992

Just as destructive and inhibiting as poverty may well be the social stereotypes of what 'old people' can do. For these people, as for younger women, there are established social conventions of 'appropriate' leisure-time behaviour to constrain the ambitions of 'Hell's Grannies'. Indeed, immobility and a reduced access to motor transport may well be one of the most frustrating limitations on the contemporary elderly. Giving up the car, or relying on a deteriorating public transport system, has for most proved a severe reduction in leisure opportunities. For many, the fears of venturing out, particularly after dark, constrain activities because of suspected violence or poor physical mobility.

For those living in older neighbourhoods in deteriorating areas of cities there may be few amenities available. The elderly, like the poor, attract little investment once participation in 'mainstream' activities has fallen. The one strength of this group may be that of the ballot box, simply through growing force of numbers (18.7 per cent of the population over pensionable age in 1991, increasing from 17.7 per cent in 1981). In this way the power of the 'wrinklies' or 'grey power' may be utilized to ensure that increasing attention is directed to the generations of the ageing hippies and real Rolling Stones increasingly finding themselves on the 'wrong' side of 50, or even 75.

Unemployed

Economic and social change has ensured that the numbers of unemployed are likely to remain large in most western societies. Whether redundant through job loss or plant closure or simply part of what some commentators have seen as an unwanted labour pool, this group contains large numbers of young people and may even represent a self-perpetuating underclass enduring 'enforced leisure'.

There is frequently a direct association of unemployment with a deprived and deteriorating environment on badly designed 'sink' housing estates or in parts of the run-down inner city. The leisure activities available through spending power or existing local facilities are likely to be few in number and poor in quality. Lacking funds, having plenty of 'free' time, it is hard for young people in such circumstances to maintain motivation and direction. Authorities have always been concerned with the possible consequences for urban disorder from such potentially volatile groups. Concern with youth sub-cultural behaviour, or activity seen as criminal, has often been an important element in state intervention in such areas.

The environmental link that some have emphasized, with poor or problematic behaviour seen as reflecting the badly designed and constructed, alienating housing environment, probably assumes too deterministic a link between people and place. However, it is hard to overestimate the influence of disruptive peers and a general ethos of neglect, indifference and alienating apathy. Continuing poverty engenders growing and perpetual welfare dependence of a spirit-sapping kind. In a materialistic, acquisitive society that promotes aspirations far beyond the limited life-chances of the unemployed it is perhaps not surprising that for some young people the only rational response is to take by crime what is denied by society. So, for a growing minority, life in a depressed environment may be relieved through the excitement of drugs, alcohol, theft or potentially lethal 'joy riding'.

Whether blame is located in wider society, on the deprived communities, their peer groups, families or the deviant young themselves, depends on which social philosophy is adopted when one is confronted by social problems. The danger is that for a growing minority such a leisure environment remains a daily reality. Criminal activity may be the response of only a disruptive few, but the reality of endless time-filling television for the apathetic majority is hardly any more socially productive or creative. This deprived group provides a growing social problem for all governments as technological and economic change reduces the opportunities and resources for large numbers of the potential unskilled and semi-skilled labour force and generates seemingly endless unwelcome free time in a depressed and depressing environment.

Disabled

For those less able physically or mentally there are additional barriers to leisure-activity participation in addition to those linked with poverty. Public perception of disability tends to segregate the disabled through reducing access. Some is through thoughtlessness when activities or facilities are organized, planned, or constructed, and some is through public ignorance or discomfort at associating with dissimilar groups or individuals. The physical and perceptual barriers are real and serve to further inhibit the leisure opportunities of the disabled. Access, both financial and real, can be improved, but only if there is genuine support for integrating all citizens in a comprehensive leisure environment.

For all the groups discussed in this section, the barriers to full participation have varied depending on income, mobility and social attitudes. In combination these serve to restrict most severely the leisure action-space of groups and individuals in these categories, indeed they remain individuals rather than categories and experience the restrictions on opportunity in their several ways directly, and above all, personally.

Contemporary context

A further significant impact on all leisure activities, whatever people's ages, gender, ethnicity, or disability, is the cultural impact of the age in which they live. The chronological context is a crucial part of the leisure lifestyles available to individuals. Few are innovators and rebels, and most follow contemporary established fashions of dress and behaviour. To some extent increasing commodification of leisure has led to some standardization of the products commercially produced and available for consumption by participants.

Recently, there has been much speculation that we have entered an era that has been termed 'postmodernity'. This marks the end of the mass industrialization and urbanization associated with the Industrial Revolution and is represented in economic terms by the increasing proportion of employment in service, clerical and professional jobs and a decline in what became traditional 'blue-collar' work in manufacturing industry. Changes in the economic base are said to have been reflected in change in all other aspects of social and cultural life. The era of mass production has given way to more individualized, small batch production, no longer associated with the assembly-line working practices of motor companies and other mass producers.

Changes in paid work, both in its type and the growth of female employment, has been reflected in profound changes in all aspects of life. Instead of mass production and collective provision, whether in housing, transport or leisure activities, we have experienced a growth of individualism. This has been evidenced in political changes from the 1970s onwards and the increased emphasis on private consumption based on increasingly affluent individuals. Such individualism and affluence have been particularly represented in urban leisure styles.

Instead of the old social groupings based on occupation or class, theorists of postmodernity point to the growing significance of patterns of consumption and affluent lifestyles. Instead of people being working class or miners or doctors, marketing groupings like 'yuppie', 'twinky' or 'wrinkly' appeared. Such terms, whatever their meaning, emphasized groups of consumers rather than producers, particularly in leisure, which was increasingly about consumption of products in a wide range of available styles.

Alongside growing social and political individualism evolved a variety of styles of free time enjoyment. So-called postmodern niche markets developed, whether among those looking towards health, fitness and macrobiotic products, or towards the aesthetics of stripped pine furniture and country-cottage style fabrics drawn from a bygone age. Above all, what was seen to be available was an almost infinite diversity of styles, from high tech to rural cottage, from high calorific indulgence to the aesthetic and spare: in effect, fashions rather than fashion. Some of the diversity was available through the application of computers to design and production, allowing niches to be filled without sacrificing productive efficiency. Other aspects were due to the growth of retailing to provide a cornucopia of varied products in every high street and superstore.

This range of styles, individual diversity, and prolifer-ation of fashions has had considerable impact on leisure lifestyles and their environmental context. Each postmodern niche has its own setting, whether in the gym, sports hall, marina, shopping mall or her-itage centre. Changing leisure lifestyles, whether born out of constraint or opportunity have been as diverse as the domestic fireside to the national park. The leisure environment has to span such changes and profusion.

Contemporary leisure and policy-making

The postmodern emphasis on leisure diversity, market segmentation and social polarization incorpo-rates a growing significance of lifestyles and quality of life for individuals and society. As employment has switched towards clerical and service provision that section of the labour force, more educated and more affluent, has come to demand a high quality environ-ment for free time and general living. This demand, and the increasing competition between cities in attempting to attract whatever investment is available in recession-hit economies, ensures that leisure envi-ronments are politically important.

Civic authorities attempt to boost local economies through investment in a range of infrastructure, from those linked to cultural events like new concert halls, theatres, performance companies, galleries and

'hallmark' festivals, to sporting events like international athletics meetings and cycle races. Positive
publicity is good for the civic image, popular with the
local electorate (if prestigious and not too expensive),
and may serve to attract outside investment (see
Chapter 4, p. 103).

Each of the major political groupings adopts a differing emphasis at local level and in central government
with regard to the leisure environment. The ideologi-
cal perspective of each of the competing political
philosophies differs according to their basic attitudes
and values.

Parties on the 'right' of the political spectrum emphasize the need for efficiency in provision and operation,
and place faith in the workings of a relatively free
market to deliver. Groups on the 'left' focus on the
need for state intervention to correct market imbal-
ances and to achieve a greater level of social justice
and equity in meeting people's leisure needs. In the
complexities of reality such distinctions become
blurred, and governmental attitudes to leisure have
always been overlain by other concerns about maintaining social order for those groups, like the young
and the unemployed, with potentially disruptive free
time on their hands (Henry and Spink, 1990).

In spite of these complications, the broad pattern of
attitudes can be summed up, as in Table 1.7. Such
philosophical positions apply whether the leisure context is urban or rural. In such issues as wildlife conservation or the operation of sports halls the same
broad approach has frequently been adopted and not
always successfully. Leisure policy in the environment has varied between the limitations imposed by
reliance on local and state bureaucracies in the man-
agerialist allocation of resources, to the equally dog-
matic reliance on the market despite its sometimes
anarchic consequences and its failure to account ade-
quately for social costs and benefits. As the political

context has changed, so has the emphasis, more bureaucratic in the 1970s, or more market oriented from the 1980s onward.

Table 1.7 Political philosophies of leisure and environment

	Policy aims	Policy means
LIBERAL–INDIVIDUALIST	Ensure open market to give efficient operation and use of resources Limited state subsidy or intervention	Private operation and provision run competitively Public contracts only where essential
CONSERVATIVE	Maintain traditions, values and lifestyles through healthy and wholesome recreation in appropriate settings	Assist established forms and organizations to maintain culture, sports and lifestyles
REFORMIST	Greater equality of access Benefits of leisure available to all Freedom by state action correcting market imbalance	State intervention, planning and subsidy
MARXIST	Leisure rights established by state	State provision based on needs

The result in the 1990s has been the shrinkage of the public sector through restricted investment and the imposition of compulsory competitive tendering for service provision. The limited extent of development activity taking place in recession has tended to be based on private sector capital. Given the orientation of the liberal–individualist philosophy that has dominated the New Right policies of Thatcherism and beyond, it is perhaps not surprising that the social polarization described earlier as a part of postmodernity has been perpetuated and entrenched in leisure as in all other facets of social life. The disadvantaged discussed earlier in this chapter have not had the potential effective demand to be attractive to market operators, and so those populations and the parts of the city and rural areas they inhabit have had to rely on a shrinking pool of public investment and provision (Henry, 1993).

The divisions of society have been as real in leisure as in all other aspects of the 'dual' city or the impoverished countryside, and in discussing the leisured lifestyles of the two-thirds who are car- and home owners, the other third should not be forgotten. In the 1990s leisure on the 'sink' council estate or the village filled with rural elderly is as restricted and constrained as ever. Its contrast with the benefits of the rest of society is thus even more noticeable.

Questions and exercises

1 How important is access to a car for your leisure activities? What restrictions would reliance on public transport place upon your chosen pursuits?
2 How has leisure spending in your household changed recently? What are the factors that have influenced this pattern? How many of the changes are related to changing levels of income?
3 What 'concessions' are available for particular social groups at local leisure centres and other public facilities? How are these related to spare capacity or off-peak times, and how far do they marginalize or even stigmatize such users?
4 Have you experienced constraints on your leisure activities as a consequence of particular social attitudes or discrimination? What form does the restriction take, and can you fight or reduce it?
5 How important do you consider the context of people's 'formative' years for the orientation of their leisure tastes and styles? To what extent are parental or even grandparental activities and attitudes to leisure the product of their adolescent years rather than contemporary opportunities and context?
6 Do you associate current diversity of leisure styles with growing individualism in economy and society? To what extent have fashions taken over from fash

ion in popular music or clothes?
7 Has your local council used leisure, sporting and cultural events to boost the image of the local area? What types of event have been promoted and how has the civic image been changed?
8 How does the political allegiance of your local council influence its approach to leisure provision? Would change of local political control make any major difference to attitude, investment or leisure opportunities?

Further reading

The most useful source of contemporary data on economy, population, households and leisure activity, remains, as this chapter has evidenced, the *Social Trends* volumes produced annually by the Central Statistical Office, since they provide an accessible, comprehensive and regular review of most relevant aspects of social life. This breadth of treatment of leisure in contemporary society is also to be found in texts like Les Haywood *et al.* 1989, *Understanding Leisure*, or historically in John Clarke and Chas Critcher (1985) *The Devil Makes Work: Leisure in Capitalist Britain.*

For the leisure opportunities of particular social groups, read texts like Rosemary Deem (1986) *All Work and No Play? A Sociology of Women and Leisure,* or E. Green *et al.* (1990) *Women's Leisure? What Leisure?* or more on general urban action-space, Little, Peake and Richardson, eds (1988) *Women in Cities.* The implications for the unemployed are comprehensively explored in Sue Glyptis (1989) *Leisure and Unemployment.*

Changes in the cultural and the political context are addressed in Ian Henry (1993) *The Politics of Leisure Policy,* and in Mike Featherstone (1991) *Consumer Culture and Postmodernism.*

Leisure in urban areas

2

Spatial distribution of activity

When we look at urban areas and make any kind of inventory of their leisure facilities, it soon becomes apparent that activities and the necessary facilities are not randomly distributed, but conform to a general pattern affecting land and property throughout the built environment. In some urban settings we expect to find fashionable boutiques and up-market eating and drinking places, while in others the run-down shops and glass-strewn 'green' spaces lack both functional and visual amenity. Some places resonate with prosperity and life, while others are quiet backwaters of residential peace.

This sorting of activities and facilities is as real for leisure, as for all other facets of living, as people seek, and others provide, particular spaces to fulfil objectives of successful commerce or satisfactory enjoyment. Whether we are users or providers, customers or managers, clients or professionals, the setting is part of the wider urban context and conforms to the general ordering of urban experiences within the built environment.

Leisure activities in urban areas have always been located according to their competitiveness in a profitable marketplace for land and property. Historically, such competition has been theorized by a number of urban economists attempting to relate the developed pattern to underlying relationships with profitability and operating costs. Alonso developed a series of bid-rent curves for different urban land-users dependent

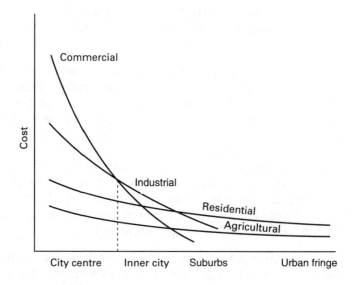

Figure 2.1 Generalized bid-rent curves (after Alonso)

on their need for a central highly profitable location. The main advantage of such a theory (see Figure 2.1) is that it alerts us to the relative competitiveness of activities associated with the use of land at varying levels of intensity.

Commerce, according to this approach, would require a highly accessible or prestigious central site in order to attract a large potential client group, and would use this expensive land quite intensively in order to generate sufficient revenue and, ultimately, profits. Industry, with less pressing need for a city-centre location, would nonetheless, at least historically, seek access to rail facilities, industrial premises or a local labour force with which to operate efficiently and profitably. Residential users seeking greater peace, greenness and traffic-free areas would favour sites giving satisfaction rather than profitability, and hence would favour distancing themselves from the hustle and bustle of commerce and industry. Agriculture, with a low level of intensity and profitability of use, would necessarily be relegated to areas not in demand from other users, and hence be peripherally located.

Within this 'pecking order' it becomes apparent that competitive and prosperous uses can replace less profitable activities. Businesses can buy out houses for conversion into commercial premises, houses replace agricultural crop-land, and so on. The only obstacle to such progression is the regulation of this land and property market by the state, both locally and nationally, through a system of zoning in town and country planning. In this way residential and agricultural land or open space may be protected through local plans that prevent commercial development.

The economic pressures to develop locations remain, and commercial decisions and residential preferences operate to create a pattern of more and less desirable sites and buildings that can only partly be modified through town planning. The distribution of activities, however, is not as regular as the theory would lead us to believe. There are vacant sites, derelict plots and run-down buildings, as well as trends as to where people wish to live and play.

Increasingly, the old pattern of access has been changed by the car, so that city centres may now be harder to reach than ring road or motorway sites. Accordingly, the rent or value of peripheral sites rises relative to the cost of a run-down inner urban setting. In most cases urban sites have already been developed, so it is existing real estate or buildings that are being rented or bought. The condition and usefulness of the existing property on any site is likely to be the most significant factor in determining its value. Thus the simplified model (Figure 2.1) only very partially describes what is going on in urban areas, and we need to remember its limitations.

The reality is less of a 'market' when only a small proportion of properties are available at any time and where the competing bidders for them have very different objectives for their future use. Particularly in leisure activities the nature and objective of the user covers a huge spectrum of profitability, turnover, clients, markets, accessibility, intensity of use, and so on. The very diversity of 'leisure' means that no single label, whether commercial, industrial, residential or agricultural, can easily fit the day-to-day reality of urban land and property allocation. However, there remains a broad patterning of uses that corresponds to some extent to the need for profitability, the extensive use of land, or the search for quiet and less expensive satisfaction. This gives us the broad pattern of leisure in urban areas to which we have become accustomed.

The broad distribution of leisure uses may be tabulated as shown in Table.2.1.

Table. 2.1 Pattern of urban leisure environments

	Activities	*Facilities*	*Conflicts*

City centre	Shopping
	Dining and
	  drinking
	Tourism
	Plays and films
		Stores
		Boutiques
		Malls, plazas and
		  precincts
		Cinemas and
		  theatres
		Bars
		Restaurants and
		  fast food
		Galleries,
		  museums and
		  libraries
			Commercial
			  competition
			Profitability or
			  subsidy

Inner city	[Poorer lifestyles]
	Living
	Shopping
	Local recreation
		Small shops and
		  video outlets
		Terraced houses
		Traditional parks
		  and residual
		  features
		Pubs and clubs
		Take-away food
		Bingo
			Competition
			Uneconomic local
			  market
			Poverty area

	Activities	Facilities	Conflicts
Suburbs	[Family housing] Living Shopping Local recreation Private sports clubs Walking	Housing estates [lower density] District shopping centres and parades Hotels Restaurants Pubs and clubs Tennis, cricket, soccer facilities Larger parks and sports grounds	Pressures for housing and commerce Stronger political protection
Urban fringe	Walking Riding Shopping Picknicking Motorsports and riding	Country parks Green-belt areas Footpaths and bridleways Car parks Golf courses and sports fields Ring road shop sites	Conflict of user objectives Peace v noise Nature v development

Historic patterns of leisure spaces

Many of the leisure facilities in contemporary cities were developed, like the cities, in the period of rapid urbanization associated with the Industrial Revolution. In the unregulated urban growth of that period vast areas of badly constructed housing were built in close proximity to the factories whose labour force they housed. Over time, conditions were reformed and civic authorities regulated the density of housing development by limiting the number of dwellings on developed plots and by insisting on minimum street widths and better drainage and ventilation. Despite the changes, the old street and field boundaries became established and still remain in many inner urban areas. Terraced housing intermingled with a few areas of open space, often the undeveloped remnants of building plots, remains as a reminder of this period of rapid growth.

A range of leisure facilities has also survived from this era. In addition to the small pockets of open space, often incorporated in formal parks with railings, walkways and small clumps of bushes, there are the many public houses and social clubs that date from the end of the nineteenth century or early twentieth century. Some stand out as major landmarks in the mean streets they have come to dominate, and their presence reflects a continuing leisure role as a meeting place and social centre for those traditional communities still occupying this inner urban housing.

The drinking places may well be augmented by other residual facilities such as the bingo hall, often converted from a former cinema or even music hall, and the large number of churches and chapels, which also reflect a past age of higher density population and thriving congregations. These features, and the shops on street corners or clustered in short parades, make up the majority of continuing facilities. The limited range of amenities and the restricted spending power of the local population of elderly, unemployed and ethnic minorities indicates a leisure structure based on past population and prosperity that has often seen 'better days' (Spink, 1989a).

In contrast, most city centre features are equally rooted in the past, but display a far more vibrant present exploitation of their locations and premises. The nineteenth-century city established a distinctive core within its commercial heart, well served by a transport system based on horse-buses, trams and railways. Rail terminals, with their associated hotels, commercial buildings and shops, became nuclei for further development.

City centres, because of their accessibility for the rest of the city, attracted the first department stores.

These were the beginnings of the consumption surge, where middle-class ladies could shop in public places without fear and in a socially acceptable way, making full use of the comprehensive range of goods stocked by the large emporia. The development of multi-storied department stores, like Brown Muffs, Boyes, Schofields, Gammage, Dickens and Jones, Lewis's, presaged the rise of the commercialized 'down-town' and the importance of Oxford Street and its provincial equivalents for window shopping, strolling and purchasing. In addition to stores, the presence of arcades, the shopping malls of their day, reflected in their splendour substantial investment in an increasingly profitable activity.

Complementing the investment in commercial retail property was the establishment of a range of other facilities for the growing free time of citizens. Public houses, eating houses and grand restaurants, often linked to central hotels serving the growing commercial trade, made their appearance. Theatres and music halls, with the latter often catering for a more down-market clientele, became notable landmarks in most urban centres. Growing affluence and prosperity linked to Britain's colonial trade and profitable European and global markets was reflected in increased investment in the urban cores. Not just commercial interests were involved, since civic pride required that prosperity and status were demonstrated through town halls, public concert halls, art galleries and museums. The quest for sobriety and industry made the latter particularly favoured by civic authorities, along with the improving influence of night schools and mechanics' institutes.

In this way a full range of leisure amenities began to be established, reflecting the growing demands of increasing urban populations. Cities could support a full spectrum of amenities. Not simply parks, often given by civic benefactors or laid out by enthusiastic authorities following Birkenhead's example, but in time the public wash-houses gave way to the full range of municipal baths. These glazed tile and wrought-iron establishments were the wonder of their age. Steam-heated for regulated swimming pools, with therapeutic baths and Turkish baths, they survived until relatively recently, closing finally through costly obsolescence.

This city central pattern of leisure activities tied to shopping, eating out, public entertainment and even self-improvement has persisted (Walvin, 1978). After the First World War, the theatres and music halls were supplemented through the appearance of cinemas. More recently there has been the growth of bowling alleys, fast-food outlets and multi-storey car parking to accommodate car-borne access, but the basic pattern has remained, though updated.

The shops have changed their frontages, and boutiques fill the old department store shells, where these survive. Many of the central streets have been pedestrianized to improve the quality of the shopping experience, and in some cases even glassed over and turned into private malls. The arcades that survived central redevelopment in the 1960s have been joined by more recent retail building, and have in some cases taken over other redundant buildings for retail use. This conversion and use of the urban fabric reflects the continuing vitality of most urban centres for leisure. The down-town area still acts as a magnet for specialized types of free time activity.

One continuing change that has affected urban centres has been the outward spread of population. The growth of suburban and rural fringe commuting to 'metropolitan villages' has been reflected in an outward distribution of leisure facilities. Dispersed populations and car-ownership have encouraged facilities to migrate outwards to take advantage of cheaper land. Not just the golf driving ranges and sports fields are located on the periphery of cities, but increasingly the ring road has become an ideal site for shopping centres and multi-screen cinemas. The trend to sub-urban living expanded after the First World War and has continued following increased car-ownership more recently. It has led to a diffusion of facilities out-wards and a less concentrated structure for the urban leisure hierarchy (Table 2.1).

The spread of the city and its functions has been remorseless, from the pedestrian-scale medieval era to the 'tracked' city of the nineteenth century and the motorway city of today. The increase in scale and diffu-sion of facilities linked to ownership and use of private cars has made physical and economic access even more differentiated and, as was seen in Chapter 1, selective. The historic development of urban areas has been based on differentiated life chances, lifestyles and qualities of life. Leisure has followed every other aspect of life in such respects.

The change in the nature and scale of the activity (see Table 2.2) has found changing expression in the urban setting over time. What began initially as a col-lective activity, produced, enjoyed and participated in locally, has increasingly been mass-produced for a large but differentiated market. Leisure, as it became increasingly commercialized and commodified, fitted the constraints of profitable production, benefiting from economies of scale, and both mass and niche markets.

Accordingly, the venues of activity have changed and the location has tended to move from the collectivities of the public sphere to a more individualized provi-sion, often in a private or domestic setting. This has led to a change in emphasis, from the public setting of town centre or marketplace in the medieval period, and later, to, more recently, the much more isolated location of individuals in their own rooms or within the confines of headphones and video screens.

Table 2.2 Changing leisure activity patterns

Period	Scale	Activity	Scope	Location
1 Medieval to early Industrial Revolution	Craft production Amateur Self and local	Mystery plays Games Band/ dances Concert party	Small group consumption	P U B L I C
2 Industrial Revolution	Commercial production Local and mass	Music halls Theatres Cinema League spectator sports	Mass collective consumption	
3 Modern	National production Mass market	Newspapers Gramophone Radio/TV broadcasting	Domestic group and individual commodity consumption	P R I V A T E
4 Post modern	Multi-national production Global scale but niche markets	Personal stereo Video CD Screen games Satellite channels Virtual reality	Individual commodity consumption	

The part played by public authorities has varied over time. Public settings were much more prone to licensing, regulation and concern over the impact on public morals, and, in consequence, more likely to receive either public investment or subsidy, to ensure the promotion of morally correct or uplifting activities. With more individualized and domestic leisure the field has been left much more to private commercial producers, with the high point of welfarist intervention coming in the late Industrial and early Modern period with its civic museums, art galleries, baths and parks, along with development of playing fields and other public amenities.

Private commercial interests have more recently met the increasing demands for individualized commodities for domestic consumption. In the branded goods produced on a global basis there has come to be an increasing assimilation and integration of cultures and artifacts, with national, regional and local production and localities of consumption becoming less and less significant.

Increasingly similar types of products bought in increasingly similar venues gives a pretence of individuality that is rarely present in reality. Modern technology in a variety of ways has diminished time and space, and the abolition of local difference has been one of the consequences of these changes. Internationalized cultures consequently dominate the postmodern stage and are part of the range of lifestyles available for individuals in a domestic setting. The switch to private provision has been matched by increasingly individualized consumption, usually around people's home bases.

Leisure in the postmodern city

As was suggested in Chapter 1, some social commentators have come to label the major changes in the structure of economy and society in the last 20 years as the era of 'postmodernity'. They have argued that the former long established phase of production, which emphasized mass production and assembly line methods and came to symbolize 'Modernity', in factories, manufacturing industry, building styles and general culture, has been supplanted by more recent changes. Instead of the focus on mass consumption, on collective provision of housing and transport, on mass entertainment forms like the cinema or spectating at professional team sports, new forms of living and recreation have taken over.

Postmodernity implies change to more flexible forms of production and profit-making associated with the rise of service industries and the decline of the old 'smoke-stack' industries. Economic changes leading to the growth of 'white-collar' and female employment have meant more than simply changes in the nature and composition of the labour force, but also in the way that people live and see themselves. Post-modernity is reflected in the city by changing lifestyles, with more emphasis on education, professional attainment, job flexibility and individuality. Economic change has been mirrored by change in culture, politics and society generally. It is argued that old allegiances based on work and class have become weaker as people increasingly associate with their life as consumers rather than producers.

This emphasis on consumption and a more individualistic leisure lifestyle has been expressed in changing leisure environments, particularly in urban areas. Greater environmental awareness and the demand for higher quality experiences, with rising general personal affluence, have led to the creation of pedestrian cores, shopping malls, and the refurbishment of down-town areas with planting schemes, new lighting and even the roofing over of shopping streets. To cope with the growth of services, more and more office blocks, with their associated restaurants and wine bars have come to dominate down-town areas. The remodelling of city centres has come to emphasize not just the upgrading of the environment but also has focused on heritage, whether industrial or historic, in an effort to please visitors, potential investors, shoppers and office workers.

Attractive features such as open spaces, old buildings, and, above all, water features, have been seized on in the drive for creative 'image' building. Riverside, dockside, or canalside buildings have seen a rapid increase in value as their image has been transformed. The linked waterside walkways have become a feature of almost all postmodern cities, along with prestige buildings, acting as landmarks or 'gateways' to the resurrected down-town areas (Harvey, 1989).

In these settings the postmodern leisure activities of shopping (consuming), window-shopping, or simply strolling while enjoying the metropolitan experience of crowds, street theatre, buskers, fast food, open-air entertaining, or simply seeing and being seen in a suitable setting, have come to dominate. The construction of these leisure 'sets' has been a vital part in the transformation of a number of cities. Allied with garden festivals, new marinas, water events, spectaculars, and so on, the image of dour industrial cities has been lifted to form that of a suitable venue for shopping, leisure trips, cultural happenings and even tourism.

All have competed for the same market of consumer spending and service industry relocation. Some have been successful, but in many the unlet shop units and vacant office floors bear testimony to the anarchy of market over-provision and continuing restructuring. Probably urban waterside areas have seen the greatest transformation in appearance and property values, along with those inner city suburbs eligible for gentrification, by that army of lower-paid service sector professionals, affording them their first step on the ladder of owner occupation. In many ways the two gentrifications fit together, since the revitalization of the city of culture, arts and entertainment is linked to the presence of nearby educated, though lower-paid, professionals who find the metropolitan ethos attractive and the inner terraces accessible, convenient and economical.

These then are the main features of recent change in economy and leisure lifestyles on town and city centres:

1 The growth of more service jobs, mostly female, and the decline of traditional manufacturing.
2 Construction of new office and shopping spaces linked to economic structural change.

3 Transformation of down-town areas through pedes-
   trianization, new street furniture and planting.
4 Emphasis on water features, whether canals,
   rivers, seafront or docks as a venue for white collar
   employment and residences for the affluent.
5 Focus on aspects of urban heritage and historic
   associations as crucial ingredients in 'image building', boosterism and promotion.

The growth of home-based leisure

Urban leisure, as the introduction pointed out, covers
a wide range of activities and participants. A broad
division between the more individual, home-based
activities and public activities designed more for mass
participation and consumption is a significant one. As
the previous section showed, the growth of individualism set in homes and a domestic environment pre-
senting a higher level of space and amenities meant
they proved an attractive leisure venue. Mass consumption, whether of sport or entertainment, has
become economically precarious and has not
attracted commercial investment on the scale it
enjoyed in the heyday of Victorian mass entertainment, with the establishment of pubs, music halls,
theatres, and professional sports grounds.

The switch from the crowds engaged in mass leisure
has been replaced by a more individualistic and frag-
mented pattern of activity. People may throng the
shopping precincts and entertainment districts of
towns but the participation is much more on an individual and small-group level. Individuals may well be
shopping, or selecting videos or games cartridges in
the public arena, only to enjoy the leisure activity
later in a more private setting. Given the pressures of
economic competition detailed earlier, it is perhaps
not surprising that, in consequence, many urban
public leisure facilities, whether variety theatres, cinemas, or dance halls, have succumbed to competition

and been unable to survive in a setting of more privatized leisure activity.

Several issues It is the spending on home-based and individual activities that has attracted growing contemporary investment (see Table 1.1). Home entertainments take a variety of forms but the majority are electronic and are reflected in the proliferation of retail outlets for audio, television and satellite channels, videos, electronic games and computing. The expansion of this highly profitable market is backed by real estate in shops in both city centres and suburbia, but the home-base remains the venue for participation.

Home improvements The home-base looms large in current retailing, not just for entertainment, but also its maintenance and improvement. The proliferation of do-it-yourself superstores and the popularity of garden centres each weekend bears testimony to the attraction of improving homes and gardens, not simply out of satisfaction, but also as a capital asset for the majority of leisure participants engaged in DIY or gardening.

Both activities may be close to the philosophical distinction between 'leisure' and 'work' but they occupy increasing numbers and amounts of free time. The popularity of these privately based and individually centred activities has meant growing commercial investment in both stores and specialist goods. Households have been prepared to spend large amounts on home improvement and gardening supplies, and this popularity with a more affluent section of society has been matched by profitability and further investment. Working on the house, the garden, or even the car or caravan, has become the weekend pursuit of 'self' improvement for millions, in contrast to the declining significance of mass participation activities formerly dominant, whether theatre-going or soccer-spectating.

Individualized leisure is represented in high streets and shopping malls in other ways. Less bulky than

DIY or garden supplies and hence represented in a host of small retail units, are pursuits like photography, country sports, jogging, fitness training and even travel agencies. All cater for expensive free time activities pursued by the relatively affluent on an individual basis, and they seek to provide a range of essential equipment or provision. Any High Street shows the proliferation of such outlets which take an increased proportion of the shop units and the spending power of households. Accordingly, even the composition of the retail outlets in any shopping centre reflects a growth of individualized and largely consumption-based and home-centred leisure activity.

The popularity of this diverse variety of solitary and small-group activities has had implications for other, often more traditional, activities. Team sports, especially those particularly demanding of time and space, like cricket, may well have lost out among the young and the paying spectator. Professional sport has not been resilient in the face of changing tastes, and declining attendances or even closure of facilities like dog-racing tracks have occurred in consequence (see Chapter 4, p. 98). There is still much physical activity, in jogging or country walks, but less localized communal activity based on neighbourhood loyalties and facilities. With more diversity of opportunity and pressures on time, it becomes harder for some 'teams' to function, and car travel has added to the range and breadth of catchments of alternative or competing recreational facilities.

Changing leisure provision

In recent years there has been a reduced amount of public funding available for investment in leisure facilities. Most British towns and cities have been, and are still, reliant on a great mass of nineteenth-century investment, not just in recreational amenities like parks, libraries, swimming baths and theatres, but also for the basic urban infrastructure of roads, sewers and buildings. The scale of past investment is still an important determinant of available opportunities, and some cities are, in consequence, far better endowed than more recently built new towns or outer estates. The nineteenth-century heritage is not always appropriate or conveniently located, but it remains as a vital legacy on a scale rarely matched today.

Current provision has increasingly come from the private sector, and so commercialized leisure activities like bowling, cinema viewing, drinking and fitness training have come to dominate. Where local authorities have been involved in the developing of facilities like stadia or leisure pools, then there has been an increasing awareness of running costs, possible revenue, and the possibility or certainty of contracted management by outside agencies. This affects design, size, staffing arrangements, and the same approach to efficiency and profitability as that adopted by the private sector.

Local authorities restricted for capital and revenue thus act increasingly like private operators, which has significant implications for access. In location, pricing and market orientation, recent ventures like swimming pools or skating rinks, whether publicly funded or joint ventures using both public and private investment, look increasingly alike. Concessionary access can only be available off-peak or at unpopular times and seasons. The market has thus come to dominate recent provision, which has implications for any kind of urban leisure policy or local strategy (Henry, 1993).

Certainly until the late 1970s there had been a real concentration within urban areas on the concept of 'standards' in leisure provision to be met by local authorities. Standards were established for distances between facilities or the availability of particular resources like playing fields. The National Playing

Fields Association established the recommendation of
6 acres (2.43 hectares) of playing space per 1000 population. The notion of standards has its advantages as
well as some disadvantages, as set out in Table 2.3.

Table 2.3 Evaluation of 'standards' approaches

Advantages	Disadvantages
Simple to understand	Questionable (various sources and assumptions
Already accepted	Abstract and invariable
Equitable	Minimum provision target
Authoritative	Dominates priorities
Measurable	Uniformity ignores quality
	Outmoded and inflexible

The most significant feature of the playing-space
standard was that it was widely accepted as a mean-
ingful figure by decision-makers, whether planners,
civil servants or councillors, and its acceptability
meant that it was widely adopted. Similar recommendations about the availability of baths, running
tracks, ice rinks, have not achieved the same currency, and so have been far less influential. Indeed,
for many facilities, instead of the notion of a level of
provision determined by distance as a basis of accessibility, it has been the idea of a minimum population
necessary to form a satisfactory catchment population which has come to dominate in an era of financial
constraints.

The 'threshold' approach is based on the minimum
number of customers necessary to keep a facility fully
used or even financially profitable. Just as major
stores need a certain number of customers to justify
opening a new branch in a particular town, so careful
research is needed to show that sufficient population
is within the catchment area of a new leisure facility,
whether public or privately funded.

This focus on markets and running costs has been
linked to the closure of smaller facilities. The

economies of scale and increased per centages of use favour fewer and larger leisure facilities of whatever type. Accordingly, one centre, whether for cinema, bowling, indoor sports, or swimming, is likely to be provided. The old welfarist notions of equality of access tend to be relegated in such locational decisions, which emphasize efficiency of operation above most other considerations. Local authorities have found themselves with less room for manoeuvre in the operation of declining recreation budgets and have come to rely increasingly on the private sector exclusively, or in joint promotions. In such an atmosphere the idealism of past leisure strategies and plans tends to be neglected. Authorities have looked to fulfil their aims in any way they can.

One approach that has been adopted in some circumstances is that of 'planning gain'. Where a commercial developer is eager to proceed with building a potentially highly profitable facility, then the local council can link the proposed development with a scheme of its own. In this way shopping developments have been allowed, provided they include locally necessary provision of facilities like libraries, health centres, theatres and swimming baths.

Clearly the leverage of the authority is linked to the potential profitability of the proposed commercial development, and in times of recession councils have found developers to be more resistant to what they see as the 'blackmail' of public provision. Planning gain has become less dependable in a highly competitive market when in most cases local authorities compete against each other to provide sites for new commercial development, particularly if it has employment potential.

The search for employment has meant that authorities look favourably on a range of private developments in the hope of job creation. Traditionally, new developments brought new jobs and established a

Figure 2.2 Urban growth circuit

circuit of growth (Figure 2.2), which acted to multiply the impact of any development out into the wider community. The concept of the 'multiplier' is still used, but the 'spin-offs', particularly when so many leisure and tourism related jobs are low-paid and part-time, are less noticeable, though still vital.

The need for local employment encourages support for schemes, in many cases despite negative impact on green belts or the environment, and in a competitive setting there can be few prospects of planning gain when commercial developments are working to tight budgets and low profit margins.The dire financial straits of many local councils explains their eagerness to support new schemes despite their impact on the environment. Continuing financial shortage seems likely to ensure that the many conflicts associated with the physical development of facilities are likely to continue.

Urban leisure conflicts

The competition for urban space described earlier has many consequences for leisure activities in that it pits different leisure uses against each other and against various other competing users of land. The more extensive and less profitable the use, like sports grounds, the weaker or more vulnerable the competitor, and, accordingly that activity may be likely to lose out in the battle for urban sites. Pressure can arise at any number of points in the pattern of leisure land use, depending largely on the economic strength of the activity in question. Strong land-using activities include bars, theme pubs, fast-food outlets, and fashion boutiques; and weak land-using activities include playing fields, theatres and informal public open spaces.

Clearly, the extent of land required, and its location and degree of profitability, are central to the economic consideration of a possible loss of facilities. However, there is also a political context to consider, since many otherwise unprofitable facilities receive a subsidy from local sources like town councils or from national agencies for sport, arts and culture. In this way, museums, libraries, art galleries and theatres survive in city-central sites against the economic odds.

Another form of political protection, in addition to direct funding subsidy, is the protection available through town and country planning legislation in the application of land use zoning. Land can be allocated for a specific type of use in a city's local plan or unitary development plan (Greed, 1993).

The designation may then be supported by the local council through its planning committee refusing permission for building development or a change of use of the land to occur. In this way established sports and leisure facilities can be maintained and the *status quo* supported. Activities continue as long as they retain political support, both locally and nationally, since developers can always appeal against a local decision by petitioning the Minister for the Environment, who has final control over planning matters.

One notable example of political support working to affect privately owned open space is that of the green belts around many British towns and cities. These areas now amount to 10 per cent of the land area of England and Wales, and reflect a desire to limit the extent of urban development. The idea of a green zone around cities is a fairly historic one, but nationally green belts were established in 1955 and have been broadly supported by public and political opinion since then. Green belts were intended both to check the urban sprawl, which was a real concern after the Second World War following the experience of the 1930s, spread of suburbia, and to provide easily accessible countryside for urban recreation. The idea of a so-called 'green lung' was first applied to London in 1938, when the outer areas were seen as potentially valuable and healthy recreation spaces close to a congested city.

Accordingly, a large number of cities subsequently adopted the concept and developed a zone of protected countryside, usually farming land, around them. Not all the consequences of this 'presumption against development' were foreseen, and not all the effects have been beneficial. Indeed, by the 1980s there were strong pressures to abandon these land use restrictions in favour of a more market-based approach to the areas, usually for house-building.

The concept of green belts has been attacked on a number of grounds. One of the main criticisms has been that, for growing urban populations, all the belts have done is to displace population outwards, leapfrogging over the undeveloped countryside, to form new growing communities further out from the city, taking countryside for bricks and mortar in just the same way as before. From this perspective, the impact of the belts is to force people to commute for longer distances and times each day, as a costly 'tax' imposed because of the existence of the city-surrounding cordon of undeveloped land.

It has been pointed out that this commuting drain on national resources has been imposed despite the belts bringing few real societal benefits. Some belts have finally been developed in pockets by persistent builders, and the real benefits have been gained by those wealthy enough to live in the protected villages encased within them.

Access to green belt land has proved to be most real for wealthy suburbanites living close to the protected countryside rather than those in the congested inner city. The notion of the 'green lung' for the congested districts has been questioned by south London evidence that a maximum of 10 per cent of users came from central city locations, while most users (75 per cent) arrived by car and lived in affluent suburbs nearby (Harrison, 1991). Certainly the greatest financial gain appears to be generated for those 'lucky' enough to inhabit large houses overlooking this protected landscape (Elson, 1986).

In places, however, the term green belt is in any case a misnomer, since the belts also include a range of derelict and marginal farming land to blight the popular image of unspoilt greenery. Despite continued public support, much of which came initially from an odd alliance of city socialists and rural conservatives, both eager to prevent excessive outward spread, it is clear that green belts have substantial negative as well as positive aspects. They have sustained areas of at least partially farmed land around cities, and maintained areas of open land for walking, golf courses, riding stables and bridleways, but at some cost to urban residents. Any restriction on the supply of land in the face of continuing demand pushes up the price of land for purchase and rent, within the restricted band. So, all urbanites have paid for green belts, whether as residents or commuters, yet their accessibility and use has clearly been greatest for affluent suburbanites.

The protection has been real but the policy, in reality, has in many aspects proved regressive – rewarding the better-off while much of the cost has been met by poorer city dwellers. Whether the protection will continue despite the pressures of a car-borne population remains to be seen. At least cars have made more of the belts accessible to a greater number of leisure participants.

Other examples of inequality in leisure provision and access are manifest in urban areas. The contrasts between the facilities and densities of building in suburban areas when compared with the inner-city are considerable. Inner-city residents, as discussed in Chapter 1, suffer the areas of smallest, most overcrowded housing, built at high densities with few open spaces, while those in suburbia have the double advantage of more space, both inside the home and around it. Not only are there private protected gardens for children's play and hobby gardening, but there also tends to be the additional advantages of more public open space in parks and playing fields, even private sports clubs, and the greater greenery of tree-lined streets, less hemmed in by housing.

All this adds up to an important advantage in the quality of environment and consequently in quality of life. The broader streets and lower density of traffic mean less polluted air and less danger to pedestrians. The coming together of radial routes and inner urban motorways takes great swathes of land in central areas of cities, while suburbanites have much less contact with a traffic-ridden environment. Many of the dense networks of central roads are, in any case, there to speed the journeys of the suburban commuters night and morning. In yet another way cities work regressively in the distribution of environmental resources like peace, safety and unpolluted air, so important for the quality of leisure time.

The car-ownership patterns discussed in Chapter 1 are significant for leisure activities, since, increasingly, there has been an outward spread of facilities and an enlargement of their catchment areas. In part this has generated more conflict in suburban districts since there have been pressures to sell off and develop lands around schools, hospital sites, playing fields, or sections of green belt accessible from major roads. There has been pressure to increase the development of suburban shopping centres, multi-screen cinemas, bowling alleys, and even swimming pools on these cheaper greenfield sites. The growth of larger, cost-effective facilities has often been accompanied by the closure of older, smaller units towards the centre of towns and cities.

Larger facilities, fewer of them, more widely spaced, with larger catchment areas and a greater minimum population size to give a profitable market, has meant longer journeys for leisure activities. The economies of scale implicit in the operation of fewer, larger centres, necessitates longer trips and hence increased costs in time and money for participants. In some cases facilities are no longer being located on bus routes, or are only served by an infrequent, expensive and deteriorating service. Greater reliance on the private car has become an essential feature of life for more people and that has had serious, socially divisive repercussions. Access to leisure facilities even in urban areas has increasingly become reliant on access to a private car, which, as Chapter 1 showed, is highly selective in terms of income, age and gender.

Maintaining parity of access to facilities has become increasingly difficult for local councils committed to continued equity in provision. The disparity of opportunity between inner-city and suburban areas has thus tended to widen as both the economic means and the physical proximity of recreational resources has diminished for the poor. Urban leisure has become increasingly about affluence and mobility, and these attributes are selectively distributed among the population. Inner-city areas with impoverished and immobile populations dependent on a limited range of poor quality and residual facilities have come to be 'left behind', in every sense, by more affluent and mobile suburbanite fellow citizens.

Questions and exercises

1 To what extent does the spatial pattern of leisure activities established in Table 2.1 apply within your town or city? Is there local evidence of a competitive sorting of leisure uses?

2 How do the leisure opportunities of the inner city come to reflect the constraints on the disadvantaged populations occupying such areas?

3 How many of the leisure facilities enjoyed in the contemporary town or city centre date from before the First World War? How many of these buildings have changed from their original function?

4 Which leisure facilities now located in the suburbs or on the edge of the urban area might once have been expected to locate on a central site?

5 To what extent do cities with which you are familiar display evidence of a postmodern transformation?

6 How much of your own leisure time is home-based? How commercialized and commodified has it become?

7 To what extent do you look to the public sector to provide for your leisure needs? Is a 'standards' approach relevant for contemporary leisure activity?

8 Are you aware of any local examples of 'planning gain' that have added to local amenities?

9 What use do you make of local green belt areas for recreation? Is the continued protection of such areas justified?

10 How would you assess the difference in leisure opportunities within an inner city and an outer suburban area with which you are familiar? How and why do the opportunities differ?

Further reading

A comprehensive exploration of urban life is provided in Paul Knox (1987) *Urban Social Geography*, which gives a social context for leisure activities. The economic implications of land use competition are assessed in Philip Kivell (1993) *Land and the City*, which reviews contemporary processes of change. The most significant account of the impact of postmodern changes on urban structure is that of David Harvey (1989) *The Condition of Postmodernity*, which contributes not only insight but also evidence from US and British cities.

Leisure in rural areas

3

The rural context

Despite the perceptions of most urban dwellers, rural areas are not without conflict and disharmony, particularly where recreation is concerned. To most townspeople the image of rural peace and tranquillity often becomes the objective of day visits and holidays in rural areas. To rural populations, eager to make a living from farming, forestry, or quarrying, the expectations of outsiders often act as a severe constraint on their economic use of the countryside. It is this diversity of use and expectation from permanent residents and temporary visitors that generates much of the conflict over recreation in rural environments.

Rural areas contain about 10 per cent of the population on 90 per cent of the land area of England and Wales. Much of the demand for recreation in these areas is thus necessarily generated by temporary visitors and tourists. Local populations are often ill-served for year-round facilities and may be deprived of recreational opportunities through poverty or inaccessibility linked to remoteness or poor rural public transport systems. Much of what is provided for recreation in rural areas is thus linked to the largely seasonal demands of tourists rather than permanent residents, and the fate of many groups in rural areas is, paradoxically, one of restricted opportunity while living in areas noted for their visitor appeal.

Some conflict between locals and visitors seems inevitable since the bulk of rural land is assigned to non-leisure uses and forms part of either the 75 per cent agricultural land or the 10 per cent forest and woodland that goes to make up the UK. Some rural areas are designated as green belt through town and country planning intervention and these currently amount to 10 per cent of the land in England, usually that immediately adjacent to the great conurbations. Other land use restrictions apply to a further 20 per cent of the UK, which has been designated as either national park (ten plus The Broads Authority), Areas of Outstanding Natural Beauty (thirty-nine), or as one of a variety of other national scenic areas (see Figure 3.1).

It is through such designation that special powers are taken by local and central government to protect and maintain a suitable leisure environment. Inevitably many of the costs involved in such zoning, the restrictions on exploitation, the additional expenditure on the aesthetic maintenance of building styles and materials, etc., fall upon indigenous rural communities, while the objectives are largely for the benefit of distant urban populations. This cost and benefit mismatch lies at the heart of many rural leisure controversies.

Just as the costs of rural conservation tend to be allocated differentially to rural populations, so the benefits of rural leisure are not shared universally within urban populations. Only about 20 per cent of the population use the countryside frequently and these tend to be under 40 years of age and are mostly from professional, car-owning groups. A further 45 per cent make occasional use of the countryside and this group of 40–60 year olds is more likely to be from clerical or skilled manual backgrounds. The 35 per cent of the population that makes only infrequent use of rural areas tends to be those disadvantaged in other aspects of leisure and life styles – the over-60s, those on low incomes and ethnic groups. Rural recreation thus tends to be selective and in many ways, in both costs and benefits, reinforces the inequalities in

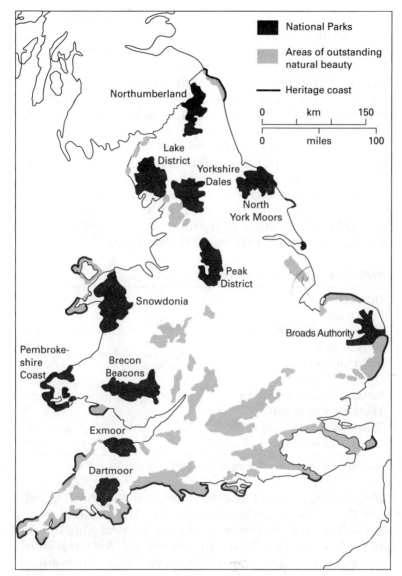

Figure 3.1 Protected areas of England and Wales

leisure discussed in Chapter 1 (Countryside Commission, 1992).

The total of 50 million visitors to the countryside each year (including 10 million visitors from overseas) may represent a narrow selection of the total population, but they present a diversity of demands on rural areas. Although most will gain access through using their private cars, few will be prepared to abandon their vehicles for the visit and most see rural areas as simply a destination for a car 'outing' or tour. Inevitable conflicts between mechanized sports and pastimes, whether trail biking, mountain biking, off-road racing or power boating, and more aesthetic or naturalistic approaches to the countryside continue to recur. However, the diversity of activities makes any official attempts to regulate or incorporate countryside recreation extremely difficult (see Table 3.1).

Table 3.1 Activities in the countryside

Drive, Outing	19 %
Long walks	14 %
Visit to family or friends	13%
Coastal visits	10%
Informal sport	10%
Organized sport	9%
Visiting historic buildings	6%
Visiting country parks	4%
Watching sport	4%
Pick-your-own fruit	2%

Source: *Countryside Commission*, 1992

Regulating a total of 1600 million visitor trips (in 1990) is necessarily difficult and the conflicts that arise from these diverse activities are probably insoluble, despite the best intentions of National Park planning boards and the Countryside Commission.

Conflicting rural land uses

The major attraction of rural areas for many urban dwellers is linked to nostalgic images of peace, tranquillity and traditional lifestyles. Accordingly, there is for many an ambivalence if not outright opposition to change and development in the countryside. The contradictory or conflicting objectives of visitors and locals are frequently expressed in the emphasis on conservation, continuity and resistance to change in the former, and the promotion of exploitation, development and dynamic change by the latter. Locals necessarily see the countryside as a place in which to live and work, while for visitors it is perceived as an environment for occasional pleasant recreation. These conflicting objectives in the use of the land generate most of the controversies associated with rural land uses.

A local population's prosperity is linked to successful farming, quarrying, forestry or even mass tourism, while for many visitors the aim is quiet aesthetic enjoyment. Examine almost any detailed Ordnance Survey map of a rural district and the intermingling of these uses of the land is readily apparent. Each land use has its own particular needs and forms of exploitation and so it is not surprising that these will frequently conflict.

As can be seen from Table 3.2, the potential for conflict is considerable and in many cases inevitable. For local residents the priority of economic prosperity brought by employment and profitable year-round land uses outweighs any difficulties of noise, possible visual intrusion, vehicle congestion or traffic danger, and ensures that rural populations are able to remain in place and their attendant services continue. The survival of rural communities is dependent on the successful operation of a range of land-using activities that often conflict with the conservationist tendencies of outsiders.

Visitors are not homogeneous in their demands on rural areas. Those seeking an aesthetic naturalistic retreat are clearly in opposition to the practitioners of mechanized sports like trail biking, off the road

Table 3.2 Rural land use conflicts

Land use	Requirements	Potential conflicts
Agriculture	Extensive area Minimum trespass Efficient profitable operation	Landscape changes Access rights Agribusiness methods Smell/visual intrusion Pollution

Quarrying	Minerals
	Efficient profitable
	  operation
	Access to markets
		Landscape destruction
		Noise/dust/visual
		  intrusion
		Heavy traffic

Forestry	Cheap extensive areas Appropriate soils	Land sterilized Access limits Habitats destroyed Landscape changed Depopulation Cropping intrusive

Water	Unpolluted
	  catchment
	Exclusivity of
	  use
		Access rights
		Land/habitats lost
		River/groundwater
		  regulation

Wind Energy	Skyline sites	Visual intrusion

Visitors/
Tourism
	Access
	
	Developed
	  infrastructure
	
	Service
	  provision
		Aesthetic or
		  mechanized use
		Individual or
		  mass aims
		Seasonality
		Conservation
		  restrictions

Housing/ Community	Land Developed infrastructure Services	Roads and traffic Conservation costs Housing competition Centralization Visitor frictions High costs/low wages

driving, water skiing or microlite flying. There are distinctions, too, in the extent to which people wish to enjoy the countryside in the company of others as a mass participation experience supported by diverse goods and services or as a solitary wilderness experience. In a highly populated and densely developed island the latter conditions become increasingly remote, scarce and marginalized.

Conflict resolution, particularly over issues of land use, has traditionally been the task of the local and central state through town and country planning legislation. This intervention has historically been much more closely focused on urban settings, with farming activities and associated landscape changes specifically excluded from the 1947 Town And Country Planning Act, under the supposition that farmers embodied reliable 'stewardship' of the land.

For much of the countryside, regulation has been limited to the physical development of village communities rather than the land directly. The only exceptions have been those areas prized so highly by urban populations, and their legislators, that they were accorded special status as National Parks (1949 Act), Green Belts (1938 London, 1955 elsewhere), Areas of Outstanding Natural Beauty (1949 Act) or some other form of protected status (Figure 3.1).

This enhanced protection has generally been utilized to conserve traditional agricultural landscape and settlement forms, and accords with the nostalgic objectives of most urban visitors. National Park planning boards frequently enforce building styles and materials from the late nineteenth century in an effort to preserve visual continuity and picturesque settings.

Such activity has been supported by the majority of citizens but it must be remembered that these constraints, and others associated with special conservation status, devolve additional costs on rural populations. The use of historic materials and craft skills rather than modern alternatives is frequently expensive, as is an antiquated road network or maintenance of traditional field boundaries. The need for a range of subsidies bears testimony to some of these costs and shows partial state recognition of the additional expenses entailed. The debate about protection and conservation continues and in many individual cases crystallizes the differing perceptions, attitudes and objectives of locals and visitors.

The resolution of the competing claims is almost impossible. It has led planning authorities like North Yorkshire County Council (1979) to identify a range of strategic planning options for its rural areas:

1 Facilitate present trends.
2 Preserve environmental quality by restricting large scale or rapid development.
3 Maximize economic potential by giving wider support for the private sector.
4 Emphasize the needs of disadvantaged groups and areas; and
5 Achieve a balance between demands and resources through integrated countryside management.

Such diverse objectives focusing on social justice or market forces reflect the wide range of political and philosophical alternatives for rural areas and their leisure uses (see Table 1.7). Authorities have to balance the issues of conservation with the demand for further visitor facilities and the economic prosperity often associated with greater exploitation, set against an environmental cost impossible to quantify.

The investigations of 'carrying capacity', landscape evaluation, cost and benefit accounting, bear testimony to the attempts to find 'scientific' and 'objective' solutions to valuational judgements. For most rural dwellers faced with increasing demands from visitors

and tourists and the need to sustain their own prosperity, the issues of sensitive development remain to
be faced as an everyday facet of countryside living.

Pressures on rural recreation areas

As noted earlier, one of the paradoxes of rural leisure
and tourism is that great numbers of urban-based
recreationists tend to damage or even destroy the very
beauty and solitude they ostensibly seek. The mass
exploitation of the countryside for leisure is a recent
phenomenon in historic terms but already has considerably damaged vulnerable and precarious landscapes and habitats.

One of the main problems has been the tendency for
visitors to concentrate on a few particularly attractive
or accessible areas that act as 'honeypots' and so are
significantly subject to visitor pressure. Visitors are
not randomly distributed across the countryside but
come to congregate at specific villages or viewpoints
and their associated car parks.

Concentrations away from the car-borne mass are
also prevalent along the lines of long-distance footpaths like the Downs Ways or the Pennine Way, which
become subject to enormous physical damage linked
to trampling by a mass of ramblers. Construction and
restoration of footpaths becomes a major task for
farmers, local authorities or National Park boards,
and the need to cope with the masses climbing alongside Malham Cove, or the 2 million walkers annually
following in Izaak Walton's footsteps in Dovedale in
the Peak District, require major and frequently incon-
gruous civil engineering projects.

Naturalists would argue that the ecology of the countryside is in any case at risk from economic development and destruction even without such visitor
pressure. Despite the limited protection of the Wildlife

and Countryside Act of 1981, the Council for the Protection of Rural England has argued that there has been a dramatic decline in natural and traditionally managed semi-natural landscapes over the past 40 years. It considers that 50 per cent of ancient deciduous woodland, 50 per cent of fens and marshes, 95 per cent of wildflower meadows, 60 per cent of lowland heaths, and 60 per cent of peatlands have been lost through development or changed farming practices. Rare species had also been lost by the 1990s, whether the red-backed shrike, the Viper's Bugloss moth and the mouse-eared bat, such losses point to irretrievable change in rural habitats and emphasize their vulnerability.

Even the Nature Conservancy Council, the government's former nature conservation advisory body, estimated that by 1990, 40 per cent of the Sites of Special Scientific Interest (SSSIs) established as 'the best examples of Britain's habitats and natural features' under the 1981 Act were deteriorating or damaged. The Council's successor, English Nature, accepted that in 1991 alone nearly 5 per cent of all such designated areas had been lost or damaged.

Given the rate of destruction it is clear that recreational use of some of the most precarious rural habitats presents a further real threat to their existence when coupled with the damage from changes in farming, road construction and building development to which they are subject. Rural recreation presents a number of challenges to the 'carrying capacity' of these sensitive environments. Visitors not only generate destruction directly through their activities, but their presence necessitates the construction of a range of infrastructure from hotels, cafés, car parks and sewerage systems which indirectly add to the pollution and destructive intrusion caused by human use.

It can be argued that the British countryside is very much a human artifact formed as a result of over

4000 years of exploitation and utilization. However, the clearing, burning, cultivation and building evolved slowly and is in no way comparable to the destructive potential of contemporary mass rural recreation (see Table 3.3).

Table 3.3 Ecological impacts of leisure use

Ecology	Recreational uses	Impact
Vegetational Habitats (moors, heaths, fens, deciduous woodland, etc.)	Rambling Hiking Camping Mechanized sport Climbing	Habitat destruction and damage from access and trampling Development of roads, buildings and visitor infrastructure
Wildlife Habitats (nest sites, dens, colonies, feeding sites, etc.)	Rambling Hunting Intrusive naturalism, birdwatching, specimen collecting Mechanized sport	Impact of human presence Disturbance and destruction Pollution (exhausts, sewage, refuse, etc.)
Landscape Features (woodland, walls, paths, dwellings, etc.)	Sightseeing Touring Hiking Mechanized sport	Visitor damage Construction of facilities and infrastructure

Politics of rural recreation

The pressures on rural environments and the inherent conflicts associated with the diversity of land uses means that leisure activities in the countryside are highly contentious and frequently politicized, with a range of interested parties. The illusory image of peace and harmony possessed by outsiders mentioned earlier in this chapter has been powerfully explored by authors like Raymond Williams (1973).

Historically, the countryside has frequently been the focus of dispute, whether over the enclosure of commons, or the destruction of villages and the usurpation of commoners' rights. In many cases the leisure of elite groups, in exclusively royal or noble deer parks and hunting forests, has been at the expense of lower orders in a feudal hierarchy. Many would argue that property rights over grouse moors, river courses, fields and forests still constrain the leisure activities of the majority.

In the past the mass trespass movement of the 1930s led by activists like Benny Rothman and the British Workers' Sports Federation, served to raise public awareness and ultimately influenced the National Parks and Access to the Countryside Act of 1949 (Shoard, 1987). Disputes over access continue, with mass trespasses in the 1990s organized by the Ramblers Association under the banner of 'Forbidden Britain', aroused by concerns that the privatization of the water industry and the Forestry Commission will reduce public access rights on private land.

With the sale of over 250,000 acres of Forestry Commission woodland since 1981, there are real fears that private owners will seek to restrict public access, and that commercial pressures will further diminish the stock of available countryside.

Access to scarce countryside may, in this way, increasingly become another source of private wealth. There are already charges for visiting sites like the Swallow Falls or High Force, and commercialized access, or footpaths provided in return for tax concessions, represent a diminution of ideas of rural space as a 'free good'. The impact of these exclusionary changes and similar reductions in collective spaces parallels the effects in urban areas of the proliferation of private shopping centres and malls. Each leads to an increasing demarcation of public from private spaces.

These changes in ownership and attitude may be further exacerbated by current governmental pressures to criminalize trespass. In an effort to deal with perceived legal 'problems' with squatters, gypsies and 'New Age' travellers, the focus of actions for trespass will no longer be a matter for civil courts, with substantial costs for the landowners concerned, but will be the domain of the criminal law and hence enforced by police directly. It is in response to such change that access has remained a high profile political issue in rural areas.

Continuing conflict over access has been an important and in many ways a typical dispute affecting use of the countryside. Other conflicts over blood sports, rural development, agricultural subsidy, and many other topics fit a general pattern. Disputes have been taken up by a variety of pressure groups that have competed for public attention and political support. In a pluralist model of democratic politics groups win general public support, and ultimately their objectives and values come to be reflected in legislation.

Pressure groups can be divided into those representing particular sectional interests directly (see Table 3.4), and those seeking to promote a particular cause, whether conservation or animal welfare, by raising public consciousness and by entering popular debate and influencing political agendas. Such groups differ in their access to the levers of power in central government, the civil service and parliament.

Insider groups may well be influential in that their views are sought by ministries, public inquiries, royal commissions and the mass media, and incorporated into legislation or government policy. Some of these groups are so close to government through funding, research grants or indirect financial support that they have little independence and are held 'prisoner' by their links with official power. Other groups are necessarily outside the realm of 'respectable' politics and may trade-off the lack of official funding and large resources for the freedom of direct action, whether the disruption is lawful or not, in pursuit of a cleaner environment or animal welfare.

Clearly there are enormous differences in the power possessed by the various groups and the idea of a plurality of interest groups competing for public support in an equal democratic arena needs to be questioned. Support by the mass media is essential if concerns are to be placed before the general public and the initiation of policy change begun, and considerable resources, both political and financial will need to be mobilized to ensure a successful outcome.

Table 3.2 Rural pressure groups

Interest groups	*Insider*	*Outsider*
	National Farmers Union	Union of Agricultural Workers
	Water companies	Inshore fishermen
	Country Landowners Association	Hill farmers
Promotional groups	Countryside Commission	Friends of the Earth
	National Trust	Ramblers Association
	Council for the Protection of Rural England	Greenpeace
		Hunt saboteurs
	RSPCA	Animal Liberation Front

Some issues and groups find such access to public consciousness far easier than others, and the channels of communication and the attitude of government are rarely neutral. Major established interests come into all important rural issues, so change in access agreements, animal and environmental protection, or agricultural subsidy takes place slowly and generates much heated debate.

Vested interests are as strong in the countryside as elsewhere. (Cynics examining the limitations of the

1981 Wildlife and Countryside Act may reflect that 75 per cent of the Thatcher Cabinet responsible for the legislation owned rural land.) The major institutions, whether statutory, like the National Park planning boards, or the Countryside Commission, or voluntary, like the National Trust (almost 2.5 million members), prefer consensus, cooperation and compromise in their dealings with rural interests. With such attitudes it is perhaps not surprising that rural leisure environments change only gradually despite the many conflicts and disharmonies encountered.

Rural diversity

Although it is tempting to think of a single phenomenon as rural leisure and recreation, there is as much diversity in the countryside as within urban areas. The patterns of leisure use and the nature of the issues associated with green belts and the 'rurban' fringe are very different from those of the remote uplands of poor agriculture and population loss. The single unifying theme is the pressure of urban populations, though this is manifest in different ways in different settings.

For areas immediately adjacent to large urbanized populations the threat of physical development is frequently the most imminent. As discussed in Chapter 2, such areas are dependent on protection through green-belt status and the resolution of town and country planning authorities to resist applications for new building and changes of use.

Pressures on these areas have grown, due in part to the congestion of many city centres but also to the increasing accessibility of out of centre locations for car-borne users. Whether for superstores, multi-screen cinemas, business parks or industrial estates, locations on the bypass, the ring road or just off the motorway link represent valuable real estate to landowners and developers if the zoning designation can be changed to a more profitable land use. In times of recession and civic competition for investment the promise of new employment is hard for many local authorities to resist.

Semi-rural sites served by good road access have advantages of access, ease of construction, and fit the extensive site demands of large-scale, low-rise development. In many cases the agricultural use being threatened is no longer profitable or is subject to problems of vandalism or trespass. In such circumstances it is not surprising that farmers seek to convert agricultural land values into commercial ones through gaining development permission. The result has been a steady encroachment onto countryside surrounding towns and cities driven by urban expansion.

The decentralization of urban populations affects leisure activities similarly. Green spaces are lost to 'executive-style' residential estates as housing expands outwards. Around many urban centres new golf courses present a suburbanized rather than a traditional cultural landscape. Populations local to these green belts are those most likely to make use of the 120,000 miles of footpaths and bridleways in England and Wales. These rights of way are the ones used most intensively, wherever car parking allows greater use by urbanites. The areas around cities soak up large amounts of countryside recreation whether for rambling, short car trips, mountain biking, or even horse riding associated with the increasing areas of paddocks and stabling devoted to 'horsiculture'.

Villages in this intermediate belt are those most attractive to urban commuter populations, and the attraction is reflected in house and cottage prices that no 'locals' can afford. Green-belt legislation has limited the expansion of many commuter villages, and that has had a number of consequences. Not only has it increased the scarcity value of existing properties and enhanced their attraction to bucolic, nostalgic commuters, but in the case of the largest centres, like London, it has encouraged and necessitated a 'leapfrogging' outwards beyond the green belt to develop village centres as far away as Peterborough and beyond.

The additional distance generated by the 'sterilization' of space for residential use is, in effect, a tax on those commuting across the belt. The additional daily mileage is expensive and time consuming and the protected spaces may be neither very 'green' nor used for recreation by the majority of urban populations (see Chapter 2) The differential benefits and the cost allocation mean that the still popular concept of green belts may well be socially regressive in rewarding suburbanites and 'stockbroker' villagers at the expense of inner urban renters and long-distance commuters (Elson, 1986; Greed, 1993).

The pressures of decentralizing urban populations which green belts were meant to withstand, have impact far wider than a single suburban zone. Long-distance commuting has for many become a feature of everyday life, recorded in an increasing journey to work distance documented by each successive census. To the individual this reduces the amount of 'free time' available outside working time, as many hours are spent in travelling, though perhaps mitigated by personal stereos or in-car audio systems. The reality of such commuting means that there are few communities in lowland Britain that have escaped some element of suburbanization and the dissipation of more traditional patterns of village and cultural continuity.

Outsiders necessarily change the rhythm and values of village life, and by workaday necessity can participate only peripherally and sometimes intrusively in their adopted 'communities'. Commuting, like second homes, forces up housing prices and disturbs the possibility of lower-paid workers continuing to occupy village residences. Mobility thus diminishes continuity and the extended village family, with a series of consequences for lifestyles and culture. The attraction, however, remains.

British urbanites have shown a continuing desire to join the landed aristocracy or ape the squirearchy. Whether in the purchase of four-wheel drive vehicles or the green 'wellies' and Barbour jackets, the call of the rural setting persists, perhaps continuing the long tradition of British anti-urbanism. The rural idyll or ideal dominates the choice of the affluent and the design pattern-books of the volume housebuilders, and ensures the development of an ever enlarged suburbia and a shrinking truly rural domain.

Rurality, beyond the range of the executive commuter, occupies the more remote areas of the UK. The pressures of urban populations are here much more seasonal than within the suburbanized growing country-town catchments of lowland Britain. Some of the remote areas have attracted greater protection through conservationist designations as national parks or recognition of other landscape or heritage assets. In these areas there is a real conflict of interest between the pressures for development in order to sustain the prosperity of local economies, and hence the presence of local populations, and the needs and perceptions of urban populations for their leisure time.

The conflicts addressed earlier in this chapter between differing land uses are in large measure due to the leisure use of remote upland areas. The emphasis on preservation of a perhaps imagined nineteenth-century landscape in an almost 'theme park' manner inhibits the activity of local residents and exasperates many. The conflicting pressures of rural use and leisure uses persist and generate continuing political controversy. The long-term economic prosperity of such marginal and peripheral areas is fragile, and in agriculture, mining, quarrying, forestry, industry and the landed estates, decline in employment has led to long-term depopulation.

Leisure and tourism represent one economic opportunity for many of these remote districts but at a price. To some extent the demand for an unspoilt environment is incompatible with other users and ensures continuing underdevelopment and the absence of an alternative future. Many of the jobs created are low-paid, part-time or highly seasonal and so the net out-migration of the young and the able continues.

Population decline is further encouraged by the attraction of these areas for over 350,000 second-home owners who help to price-out local buyers. With the loss of year-round residents there is an immediate threat to services, whether transport, medical, retail or educational. The loss of the village post office, or even more importantly, the school, helps to dissuade indigenous young families from staying. The loss of services has not been assisted by the drive for economies of scale in public provision, which has led to the centralization of secondary schools and medical centres in fewer, larger and hence more distant units.

Rural pressures and the response to them are listed in Table 3.5.

Seasonality and economic decline help reinforce the dependence on leisure and tourism for many of these areas, particularly as their agriculture, always marginal, seems likely to receive a diminishing subsidy. In some cases depopulation and abandonment of traditional hill farms and crofts threatens the very landscape features of walls, farming and vegetation patterns that urban visitors have come to appreciate and expect. Perhaps the next stage of subsidy is simply to maintain such farms and traditions for leisure

Table 3.5 Rural development pressures and state response

Location	Pressures	Response
SUBURBAN FRINGE	Development – construction and exploitation by commercial, retail, industrial, residential and recreational uses Leisure use – rambles, golf, riding, car trips, by local more affluent urbanites	Local plans Green-belt designation
RURAL AREAS	Development by agribusiness and commuter village expansion Divided communities – more mobility, diversity, and less continuity through partial suburbanization by long distance commuters Leisure and retirement use	County plans Some designation AONB SSSI ESA etc.
REMOTE AREAS	Conservation versus rural development interests (to offset economic decline and depopulation) Seasonal leisure influx– mass visitor and tourist flows Second homes fragmenting traditional communities	Conservation designation – national parks, Heritage Coasts, AONB County plans

heritage use alone rather than for any real agricultural purpose (see Chapter 4, p. 87). Maintaining the integrity of such communities and economies as little more than a gigantic theme park or open-air folk museum will present other issues of conflict and conservation.

The range of pressures explored in this section all stem from a countryside coping with the differing demands of urbanites, whether those associated with suburban lifestyles, commuting patterns, or occasional visits. In each area, however remote, the pressures exerted by urban populations are real, and represent the greatest single issue within each living environment. Coping with urban populations remains central to rural recreation and the continued well-being of the countryside.

Questions and exercises

1 Should rural populations continue to bear the costs of providing recreational opportunities for urban populations?
2 What 'rights' of access to rural land do you consider reasonable? How important is the freedom to roam the countryside?
3 Which other pressure groups concerned with countryside recreational issues would you place in Table 3.4? If you are a member of a campaigning group, what is its rural manifesto?
4 Why do semi-rural environments prove so attractive as residential bases for urban commuters?
5 What examples of rural conflicts between locals, newcomers or recreational visitors have you encountered?
6 Must the town inevitably 'swamp' the countryside?

Further reading

The most recent comprehensive accounts of rural leisure spaces and their management are contained in Sue Glyptis (1991) *Countryside Recreation*, and in Carolyn Harrison (1991) *Countryside Recreation in a Changing Society*. Current initiatives are publicized in *Countryside*, the bi-monthly newspaper of the Countryside Commission. For details of the fight for access, see Marion Shoard (1987) *This Land is Our Land*.

Issues, problems and practice

4

Previous sections of this text have examined the changing pressures and factors influencing the contemporary leisure environment. Some leisure takes place in traditional and expected settings, whether public parks, art galleries or national parks. Increasingly, however, the diversity and segmentation of leisure pursuits has come to encompass a whole range of activities and settings that would not formerly have been discernibly 'leisured'. Changing influences of catchments, participants, costs and competition have also resulted in changing fortunes for leisure activities and their venues. Accordingly, this chapter will explore some aspects of recent change through a series of topics that reflect current trends in participation and the enjoyment of free time.

'Shopping for fun': the growth of major retail centres

The post-war period has enabled an ever larger section of the population to enjoy rising standards of living. One aspect of the changed economic structure explored earlier in discussions of postmodernity has been the way in which these rising incomes, expectations and aspirations have been translated into consumption expenditure. In a prosperous and peace-time economy massive consumption has been facilitated and encouraged by governments and financial institutions as a vital part of macro-economic policy. Partly financed through post-war Keynesian welfarist spending and more recently by economic and political individualism, the consequence has been a growing potential for spending on household consumption and leisure goods. Not surprisingly, the infrastructure has developed to accommodate this potential demand.

Shopping, which in more austere days was a regular and functional necessity, has increasingly become an occasional pleasurable indulgence. Traditional daily or weekly spending on everyday comestibles and household goods has been replaced by more infrequent larger scale forays to supermarkets. Buying a few immediate items at the corner shop has been replaced, for most households, by the bulk purchase of a trolley load of weekly groceries. Necessitated in part by changing household patterns as more women are in full time employment (labour force ratio male:female 1951 of 70:30; 1981 60:40; 1991 52:48; 1995 estimate 50:50), and in part facilitated by the technology of home freezing and refrigeration, the large multiple chains such as Sainsbury, Asda and Tesco have come to dominate the market for over 75 per cent of all grocery purchases.

As a free time activity, rather than an expected part of 'housework', it is argued, such shopping has had to become a more pleasurable experience and also has come to incorporate more members of the household as willing participants. Both the role of consumption as part of the creation and reaffirmation of identity in a postmodern consumer culture, and the improving shopping environments, have worked to sustain this as a leisure-time activity for many. The bulk shopping trip has thus become an essential, even central, feature of contemporary life, and reflects the home and car-centred nature of both lifestyles and leisure styles, discussed in Chapters 1 and 2.

For the majority of affluent suburbanites and urban car-owners the nature of leisure shopping trips is best exemplified by the hypermarket scale out-of-town shopping centre. Frequently sited at the periphery of conurbations, such locations offer easier access than the congested centres of the public-transport-based nineteenth- and early twentieth-century cities. For developers they offer the opportunity to create a purpose built, spacious 'consumer palace', with ample car parking and good access for customers and distribution vehicles. Within a single mall or shopping complex the operators can provide a high quality and relatively pleasurable consumer experience, with all the eye-catching advantages of opulent planting, water features, glass-sided wall-climber lifts, atria, sculptures, terrazzo flooring, and other evidence of conspicuous construction.

The large out-of-town centre offers a safe, patrolled, vandal- and litter-free experience for the more affluent and committed postmodern hedonists. Sections of the malls can be 'themed' to overcome the obvious sameness engendered by internationally uniform shopfronts. In this controlled environment, under surveillance from countless video cameras, the barrier between shop and pavement is easily abandoned and interiors become more accessible and available. What is offered is clearly a pleasant, worry-free experience among similarly affluent people enjoying a semi-public space at a peak density rarely encountered outside metropolitan commuting times.

However illusory the experience and superficial the welcome, such shopping has come to occupy more free time for more consumers. Even the presence of food courts serves to extend the 'dwell time' and hence the purchasing opportunities of each 'outing'. The success of these building forms across Europe and North America reflects their profitability in the early 1980s and also their continuing popularity for much of the general public.

Whether at Merry Hill, Dudley; Brent Cross, North London; Lakeside, Thurrock; MetroCentre, Gateshead; or Meadowhall, Sheffield; the leisure shopping environment is the same. Access to a major road network and ample car parking is essential. Meadowhall has 12,000 car spaces just off the M1 motorway and can draw on an estimated catchment population of 9 million within an hour's drive.

For the shopper, and this is invariably *not* a solitary expedition, the attraction is not just an expensive controlled atmosphere but also a multiplicity of conveniently sited shops. In addition to the large national name 'anchor' or 'magnet'stores, which are located at the ends of centres or malls are a host of smaller and even specialist units to give some variety and diversity. Meadowhall has 230 shops (see Figure 4.1), MetroCentre 350, while the world's largest malls in Bloomington, Minnesota, and West Edmonton, Canada, have 400 and 600 stores respectively. Each offers much more than 'simply' shopping. Leisure forms as diverse as golf, bowling, cinema-going, and discos are complemented by indoor amusement parks, a perfectly preserved Ice Age mammoth flown in from Russia (Bloomington), or a 2.5 acre indoor salt-water lake complete with dolphins, galleons and more working submarines than the Royal Canadian Navy (West Edmonton).

The malls have been rewarded by successfully attracting huge crowds since opening. Thurrock attracts over 250,000 people per week, and Meadowhall over 25 million annually (1992), as do Merry Hill and MetroCentre. These free-time venues are not just for grocery and convenience goods. Most shop units are devoted to fashion items, particularly comparison goods like clothing and jewellery, sold in both national stores and locally based boutiques. Furniture tends to need more space than the turnover in these expensive settings allows and so gets 'relegated' to less prestigious out-of-town retail parks.

Increasingly malls are occupied by wares linked directly or indirectly to leisure-time pursuits: holiday firms, photographic and audio equipment, sports goods, video games, books, sports wear, and lifestyle items, ensure that the shopping focus is not solely on mundane and household wares. Credit facilities proliferate and even in recessions ensure that a growing proportion of household or leisure spending takes place in these urban peripheral settings.

The out-of-centre location of this recent retail expansion has generated fears about the viability of town centres faced with the competition of often cheaper superstores, and even cheaper warehouse clubs. In 1983 the 1270 superstores in Britain accounted for 8.6 per cent of the retail space, but by 1992 they numbered 3500 and controlled 19 per cent of the space. The resulting store closures elsewhere and the centralization of premises on the malls has meant some empty High Street shops and may eventually threaten the viability of nearby city centres.

Local authorities reacted in the 1970s by resisting the peripheral superstores and by pedestrianizing town centres in an effort to retain or attract custom. The growth of centres in the 1980s encouraged by prosperity, profitability and a *laissez-faire* Minister for the Environment, meant that all had to follow the trend or risk being left behind in the spurt of retail expansion. Some city centres have responded by focusing more on fashion goods and the attractive dynamism of precincts, plazas and comparison shopping. Others have attempted to copy the malls and have roofed over city centre streets, as in the Victoria Quarter, Leeds, to create a private space from a formerly public thoroughfare. This kind of managed space, and action by local authorities like Reading, which has instituted a town centre manager to lift standards of environment quality, show some evidence of resisting the decentralization of spending, but the main trend continues.

Despite resistance, there is strong evidence that the leisure for more and more households is focused out-of-town, and the venue for the weekend promenade is not an urban park but a suburban shopping mall. The evidence from North America suggests that they are here to stay as a major feature of many people's leisure lives.

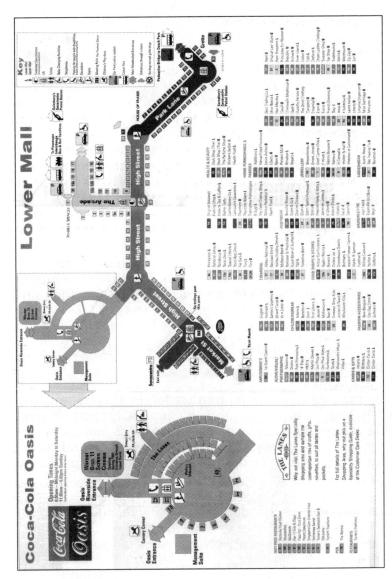

Figure 4.1 Meadowhall centre plan

Questions and exercises

1 How much of your free time is spent shopping and is it an enjoyable activity? Is it usually a solitary activity?
2 Where and when do you shop? What influences your choice of venue and how important are the surroundings?
3 Have your household shopping patterns changed? What factors may have influenced these changes?
4 Why have the out-of-town hyperstores and centres proved so popular with the general public?

Further reading

Broad aspects of contemporary consumption are considered in Mike Featherstone (1991) *Consumer Culture and Postmodernism*, and in Carl Gardner and Julie Sheppard (1989) *Consuming Passion*.

'Campaigning for space': the battle for playing space

Increasing reliance on market forces throughout the 1980s in all areas of public life has had repercussions for recreational space. As Chapter 2 noted, when development pressures are present, leisure and recreation uses, unless profitable, will be supplanted by alternative, more commercial activities.

Leisure spaces, particularly those dedicated to sporting pastimes, require extensive areas of undeveloped land and provide relatively low rates of return for that exclusive designation. In such circumstances it is not surprising that normal economic competition threatens the continuity of sports use of such areas. The threat is a direct one since many sports areas and recreational fields are particularly attractive to developers.

Relatively close to a local or urban population, playing fields are accessible and so make a good commercial proposition for retailing or land uses needing a local population catchment. Sports fields especially possess other development advantages as 'green-field' sites. They are quite extensive, particularly if there is more than one pitch, and so give economies of scale to the builder of the housing, industrial estate or whatever is to replace the turf or tarmac.

One large expanse is decidedly more valuable than a number of small, in-fill sites, and this is particularly the case in the inner city or other densely developed urban areas. The site characteristics favour ease, speed and cheapness of construction since this large, well drained, undeveloped site presents no hidden hazards of old cellars, sewers or other voids that alternative redevelopment sites may contain. If this is coupled with a good local image and a well known location then these are real advantages in economic terms and increase the 'opportunity cost' of continuing to use the space for a recreational activity bringing only a low return.

These long-standing economic and physical advantages of recreational space development were sharpened throughout the 1980s by the worsening economic circumstances of many of the owners. Whether from local councils facing reductions in grant from central government, public institutions like schools and hospitals desperate for cash, or industrial concerns needing space for expansion, car parking, or simply a capital injection from sales of assets, the threat to recreation spaces intensified.

Pressures were, if anything, increased by a central government emphasis on disposal of 'surplus' assets, which was recommended to governing bodies as more schools and hospitals became autonomous institutions. Privatization of public assets was the tone set by central government, and recreation spaces were soon placed in jeopardy by the wider dissemination of a developmental asset-stripping ethos.

Various alarm bells were rung through investigative action. In 1981 the National Playing Fields Association (NPFA), which had long campaigned for a standard 6 acres (2.43 hectares) of playing space per 1000 population, highlighted the implications of changes in directives from the Department of the Environment relating to playspace on new housing estates. The Department withdrew controls over the minimum standards covered by the Parker Morris Reports, the Housing Cost Yardstick and Circular 79/72 on Children's Playspace. These regulations and controls had ensured government direction to enforce minimum levels of provision, i.e. 20–25 square feet per person on estates, for children's play, and legitimated the financial allocation covering the additional costs of playspace provision.

As the NPFA was aware, the increasingly crude measurement of cost effectiveness of housing schemes would mean reduction in allocation by hard-pressed local authorities. With the increase in the proportion of privately constructed dwellings throughout the decade the withdrawal of recommendations and guidelines had particularly serious implications for playspace in private developments. The Department of Environment's abandonment of responsibility meant that local authority planners had little or no hope of exercising pressure on private builders to provide recreational spaces on new estates.

The official stance favouring development and reducing the necessity for recreational provision set the tone for the 1980s. Failure to provide for new sites and the threat of redevelopment of existing sites produced a double pressure that had considerable longer term implications. By 1989 the NPFA and the Central Council for Physical Recreation (CCPR) were forced to mount a public campaign to indicate the seriousness of the losses and to place playspace protection on the political agenda.

The campaign presented details of the 800 sites covering over 10,000 acres of playing space that the CCPR had registered by 1989 as threatened with development. The playing fields mostly belonged to schools, but hospitals, colleges, industrial and commercial concerns were also involved. An NPFA survey indicated that 20 per cent of planning authorities had no knowledge as to how much recreational land existed in their areas; 24 per cent had no accurate information on their land holdings and 54 per cent had no information on the dual use of educational land. With such lack of accurate information there was no way that the Sports Council's target of 3000 new or refurbished playing fields for the period 1983–8 could be quantified or even assessed.

The campaign was well organized by powerful insider groups like the NPFA, the CCPR and the Sports Council. It attracted backing for its 'Action for Play' appeal in 1990 from the Duke of Edinburgh, Members of Parliament and sports personalities and received some recognition in the resulting Planning Policy Guidance Note on Sport and Recreation (PPG 17, September 1991) issued by the Department for the Environment.

Despite the politicized campaign and the public and official support the problem has continued through the 1990s. Local newspapers continue to report the threats to sell playing fields by governors of schools, colleges and even youth organizations for housing or office park developments. Not just sports grounds are vulnerable. In 1993 English Heritage began compiling a register of municipal parks as a response to potential development threats to Victoria Gardens, Leamington Spa, and Leazes Park in Newcastle. Ironically both these threats came from recreational development for indoor bowls and Newcastle United

Football Club respectively. But local councils under acute financial pressure need to cut maintenance budgets and to generate revenue, so municipal parkland represents another vulnerable public open space asset. Its survival and that of many playing fields appears dependent on the vigilance of local communities and their willingness to campaign locally.

Perhaps the next stage of the campaign, going beyond simply maintaining playing space, will be to press for access to natural green space within and around urban areas. Access to land, water and geological features that have been naturally colonized by plants and animals is an equally important part of children's development and gives environmental satisfaction for adults.

The spread of local nature reserves bears testimony to other recreational open spaces needing support and protection. As an alternative form of urban greenery such areas can prove just as central to the quality of life and the need for sustainable cities in future. Whatever forms urban recreational spaces take, they are likely to need continued public support, both financial and political, if they are to be available as a future leisure asset.

Questions and exercises

1 Are you aware of any local examples of recreational sites threatened by development? What types of development have been proposed to replace the playing space?
2 Have any campaigns been mounted locally to oppose the loss of recreational spaces? How have the threats to the spaces been publicized and which pressure groups have objected?
3 Have local nature reserves been established in your vicinity and do they form part of an explicit strategy for sustainable recreational use of the area?

Further reading

An outline of environmental campaigning is provided in A King and S Clifford (1987) *Holding Your Ground.*

'Setting aside': agricultural change and the rural leisure environment

One of the main attractions of the countryside discussed in Chapter 3 is the appreciation of agricultural landscapes. These cultural artifacts composed of characteristic crop patterns, farm buildings, livestock and field boundaries, have gradually developed since Bronze Age times as a result of human activity. The clearance of woodland, draining of fens, expansion of ploughland and improvement of upland were crucial for farming success and the maintenance of successive rural communities. The demands of a growing industrial population and the strategic war-time concerns of twentieth-century British governments all encouraged the extensive development of agriculture and through profitability and subsidy encouraged the resulting pattern of farming appreciated by tourists and recreationists.

This established pattern of rural economy was threatened in the late 1980s by a series of proposals emanating from the European Community aimed at reducing the surplus 'mountains' of subsidy-induced produce. A number of changes to the Common Agricultural Policy were proposed in 1988 in an effort to reduce the enormous cost of storing and disposing of surplus production of butter, cereals, meats and wine. Annual payments to farmers were implemented for those prepared to forgo agricultural production and to devote land 'set-aside' from food production as fallow, forestry or alternative uses like recreation. Such major changes in farming practice would necessarily have impact on rural communities and the appearance of the countryside.

In addition to the reduction in surplus food production there were possible additional environmental benefits associated with less use of chemical fertilizers threatening wildlife and water supplies, and the opportunity of creating a number of diverse wildlife habitats. These environmental benefits have been encouraged by a series of linked grants for agricultural activity (or inactivity) and for developments that are of real benefit to conservation and recreation, such as the management of hay meadows or heather moorlands and the improvement of public access.

Initiatives like the Farm Woodland Scheme of 1988, subsequently enlarged in 1992, encouraged the creation and maintenance of new woodlands on farms to enhance the landscape and to provide an alternative productive land use. Other Ministry of Agriculture Fisheries and Food (MAFF) grants encouraged the restoration of farm buildings and field boundaries (Farm and Conservation Grant Scheme), and there were statutory codes of practice for pesticide use.

The package of measures to encourage environmentally friendly farming was linked to a more environment-sensitive Common Agricultural Policy Europe-wide, but it does not apply equally to all areas nationally. Most of the finance has been directed at those areas that have been traditionally particularly significant for recreational use and are designated by virtue of their outstanding ecological and landscape assets as Environmentally Sensitive Areas (ESAs).

The landscape, wildlife and historic features of such areas as The Broads, Pennine Dales, Somerset Levels, Shropshire Borders, Test Valley, North Kent Marshes, South Downs, and the Avon Valley have all received some additional financial support through the ESA schemes for sensitive land management. The original areas of 1987 were expanded in 1992 and 1993 to encompass further significant countryside assets, although there remains the criticism that what is needed is a nationwide scheme of environmentally beneficial land management (Countryside Commission, 1993).

In an area such as the Pennine Dales ESA the payments have been important in offsetting reductions in the livestock subsidy paid to hill farmers, and there is concern that different policies may conflict in their objectives and impact. Subsidy reductions as one element of the Common Agricultural Policy may well reduce the viability of traditional hill farming, which other grants seek to sustain. For the 700 farmers in the Pennine Dales ESA, extending from Wharfedale up to Littondale and the South Tyne Valley, the additional £2.7 million in ESA payments in 1994 proved a vital contribution to a marginal agricultural economy. The need to protect such valued rural landscapes is a real issue in areas like the Yorkshire Dales. Here the threats and conflicts outlined in Chapter 3 remain significant.

Not only is there growing pressure in the Dales from tourism and day visitors, but many settlements have been transformed by the purchase of empty farming properties for holiday homes or the retirement of middle-class town-dwellers, often seen by locals as 'permanent tourists'. The pressures on the nearby countryside are no less strong, with a highly mechanized quarrying industry and its attendant heavy traffic responding to ever increased demand. In 1992 over 4 million tonnes of gritstone and limestone were produced and mostly moved on the inadequate road network of the Yorkshire Dales National Park area. Farming changes additionally threaten the distinctive cultural landscape of the area. Redundant buildings among the more than 3000 traditionally built stone barns scattered across the Yorkshire Dales National Park present the single most important feature of the built environment, but are rarely officially protected.

Agricultural schemes like the ESA payments address some current concerns over landscape protection and conservation. Recreational enjoyment of the country-side can be enhanced by financial support for main-taining meadowland of high ecological interest and the payments for creating new public access ways in the area, or for the protection of the 3 per cent of the Dales National Park still woodland. But the long-term future of upland areas like the Yorkshire Dales remains problematic. There are a number of alterna-tive possible futures to be faced, reflecting differing objectives and political philosophies.

One would be to allow marginal agricultural areas to simply decline into picturesque decay as farms are abandoned and walls, barns and farm buildings become romantic ruins. This could be linked to the increasing role of the area as a wilderness asset as meadowland became overgrown and an increasingly natural ecology replaced the farmed landscape. 'Set-aside' payments could encourage this process of nat-ural change and ecological transformation. However, rural depopulation and a very different visitor land-scape would be created from the expected farm-managed environment of current national parks and scenic areas. Whether urban recreationists would favour such a transformation remains to be established.

Another option could be to encourage a free-market development of whatever is profitable in an unsubsi-dized rural economy. A more agri-business-centred approach might see the creation of more extensive ranch-style farming of the uplands, more forestry and the proliferation of wind-generator sites. Places could further exploit their reputation as sporting resources with the promotion of grouse or deer hunting, and for the popular 'honeypot' sites the creation of even more car parks and associated visitor amenities, like long-distance metalled paths to cope with the number of urban visitors.

Currently the extremes of free-market agricultural or recreational exploitation are being avoided through intervention schemes, National Park planning initiatives and the directed promotion of tourism, but the balance is a difficult one and the maintenance of a sustainable economically viable countryside remains critical.

The major issues for areas like the Yorkshire Dales are:

i   To maintain farming communities since these are central to the conservation of established landscapes.
ii To diversify local incomes and employment, using leisure activities and tourism as a resource.
iii To solve the problems of rural housing given the swamping of the local market by outsiders.
iv To deal with the growing quantities of traffic generated locally and by visitors.

To attempt to resolve these problems needs sensitive proactive local and central government, and sufficient range of provision to cater for the diverse demands placed upon the uplands particularly.

Many urban visitors are happy with highly managed and densely used 'honeypot' sites fringing the more sensitive and ecologically significant wilderness cores. Carrying capacity can be channelled towards those points best able to cope. Perhaps what is needed is a conscious and explicit recognition of the increasing primacy of recreational use in what are still officially seen as agricultural areas. Recognition of this dominance would allow a more constructive strategy than one based on reactionary retrenchment and the underfunded protection of declining agricultural assets.

Questions and exercises

1 How important is the maintenance of traditional agricultural landscapes to the continued recre-

ational enjoyment of the countryside?
2 Should the objectives of farming subsidy be less
  directed towards food production and more to the
  conservation of landscapes and habitats?
3 Which features of a local agricultural landscape
  would you consider worthy of conservation?
4 Do grants for landscape conservation turn the
  countryside into a series of artificially sustained
  'theme parks'?
5 Which strategy would you prefer to see pursued in
  upland areas – one favouring maintenance of traditional farming patterns or a more radical approach
  to land use and landscape?

Further reading

The issues surrounding changing agricultural and
recreational demands on rural areas are examined in
John Blunden and Nigel Curry (1988) *A Future for Our
Countryside.*

'Living with tourism': visitor pressures in the Lake District

The proportion of the British population *not* departing
on an annual holiday of at least 4 nights duration has
remained stubbornly around 40 per cent of the population for over 20 years. Whether for reasons of old
age, immobility, poverty or dislike of disruption and
new surroundings, this group is in direct contrast to
the rest of the population, who have been taking more
holidays with each passing decade. As entitlement to
paid holidays has spread to a greater number of
workers and the breaks have lengthened, so has the
holidaymaking. By 1991 over 25 per cent of the population were enjoying more than one holiday and
among professional and managerial groups that
increased to well over 40 per cent, with 25 per cent
taking at least three lengthy breaks away from home
(*Social Trends*, 1993).

This increase reflects rising affluence for much of the population despite general recessions, manufacturing job-losses, and unemployment for a substantial minority. These affluent multi-holiday households may well reflect the social divisions expressed in earlier chapters on the material aspects of postmodern society. In many cases their growing affluence is a direct consequence of at least two incomes in the household and increasing female participation in the labour market discussed earlier in the section on leisure shopping. The feminization of paid employment has brought greater spending power for two-income households in addition to greater female financial independence and perhaps recognition in 'proper' holidays of the pressures of dual roles, both domestic and economic, upon women.

More pleasurable free time has been the objective for many in their mini-breaks away from the pressures of work and the stresses of rising productivity. This growing market has led to growth in tourism and its playing an ever-increasing role in national and local economies. While tourism may represent around 5 per cent of Britain's national income compared with 30 per cent in Barbados, this growing sector has particular significance in many rural areas where alternative income may be difficult to generate or threatened by agricultural changes.

Within the UK the issues associated with growing tourism are particularly apparent in the sensitive scenic upland areas designated as national parks. One, which has historically attracted visitors from the Romantic poets onwards is the Lake District. Annually it attracts around 3 million tourists, spending an estimated £330 million, staying in accommodation provided within the 880 square-mile National Park area (English Tourist Board, 1992). This weight of tourism is clearly a mixed blessing with its costs as well as its benefits: its disadvantages to set against the positive economic contribution made to the area (see Table 4.1).

Table 4.1 Tourism impact in national parks

Benefits (+)	Costs (–)
Income	Development
Employment	Traffic
Environmental conservation	Erosion
Amenities and services	Threatened habitats
	Competition

The economic benefits of tourism are perhaps more readily apparent. A labour-intensive industry such as this contributes wages and salaries as well as the impact of visitor spending on the local economy. In an upland area like the Lake District tourism's contribution is even more valuable, for there are few other jobs and a large proportion of the workforce may otherwise be unemployed. Despite the low wages often paid there may be few alternatives and the English Tourist Board estimates that 30 per cent of employment in the Lake District is directly attributable to tourism. These service-sector jobs, in hotels, bed and breakfast accommodation, restaurants and cafés, bring further revenue into the area as rents, business profits and spending by visitors and locals are generated.

Tourist spending has a 'multiplier' effect in the local economy, since income received by local businesses is distributed locally at least in part as wages, consumption of goods, further rents, employment, profits, and so on. Despite 'leakages' out of the area in taxes, returns on outsider investment, and the cost of importing items to consume, the net economic effect is beneficial, adding to employment and spending, directly and indirectly for the resident and temporary populations of the National Park.

The income from visitors is central to the development and maintenance of many facilities, amenities and services in areas like the Lake District. Without visitor spending in a sparsely populated rural area even more small shops, post offices and bus routes would be forced to close. Summer and Bank Holiday use sustains many features that otherwise would be at risk financially, and the growth of multiple holiday breaks has increased out-of-season use and strengthened economic viability. Visitors encourage the development of local crafts in slate, rock, knitting and weaving and enable further rural diversification in a changing agricultural economy as farms develop from simply offering bed-and-breakfast-type accommodation into farm shops and the small-scale production of gourmet ice-cream, yoghurt or organic produce.

In addition to the economic development of the area and the sustenance of its infrastructure, tourism has also generated support for the preservation of the human and physical resources of the area. Although the threat of 'swamping' by an ever-increasing number of visitors is real and presents the paradox of tourism destroying itself as the sought-for environment of peace, rurality and tranquility ceases to exist, many of the visitors to the Lake District actively support the conservation of its unique cultural landscape.

The area is currently defended not only through national legislation represented by its designation in 1951 under the 1949 National Parks and Access to the Countryside Act, but in the support of the National Trust with its near 2.5 million members, and, more particularly, influential groups like the Friends of the Lake District. The popularity of the Lakes has encouraged such organizations to rally to its protection and to help to ensure, through political influence and financial contributions, that local environmental and conservation projects succeed in the maintenance of this much loved landscape.

There is, however, a negative side to all tourist development. The economic advantages are real because of the popularity of the area and the sheer numbers of visitors. This in turn necessitates the physical development of more car parks, toilets, hotels, restaurants, camping sites and all the rest of the holiday resort infrastructure. Particular centres like Windermere, Bowness or Grasmere may be able to act as 'honey-pots' and attract those who do not object to a mass-tourist experience, and who may even positively delight in it.

This development of buildings and infrastructure and the high density of usage does at least concentrate the problems of mass tourism at a few centres and leave areas of the less populous hills to the *aficiona-dos* of climbing and walking. However, the intrusion of masses of visitors and the built environment neces-sary for their support is a penalty of popularity and the growth in public access to this small area of dis-sected upland terrain.

The hills mean that local roads are narrow and tourist cars cause congestion throughout the Lake District. Local residents, farmers and businesses face growing traffic queues that lengthen tasks and add to the cost of operating in a popular area. In spite of the expendi-ture on car parks, with their visual intrusion, these can never prove adequate at peak times, and visitors frequently park unthinkingly and obstruct minor roads and gateways. All this congestion adds to the feeling that the capacity of the Lake District to accom-modate all the visitors and cars seeking entrance at peak times is increasingly being exceeded.

The lakes themselves are also subject to the pres-sures of increased use. They remain popular for water sports such as water skiing, power-boat racing, and more traditionally for swimming. Despite a speed limit of 16 km per hour, many find power-boats an intrusion and this is particularly true on Lake Windermere, where the number of fast boats has increased rapidly, producing average noise levels of 50 to 65 decibels during 1992 tests, when many local authorities regard levels above 45 decibels as unacceptable in residential areas. Boating has also added to the water pollution, not only through oil and diesel spills but also due to craft pumping sewage directly into the lake. The problems of dealing with sewage and litter are not just an aquatic issue, but a major problem for the National Park Authority throughout the district, faced with increasing visitor numbers.

Visitor pressure, whether on the network of paths across the fells or around the lake shores, threatens fragile and vulnerable eco-systems. Heavily used footpaths broaden as the grassy surface is worn away, and in places artificial surfaces have to be laid to protect surrounding vegetation and channel visitor use. The numbers of people around the lake shores for picnics, bathing or boating serve to destroy vegetation and reduce the range of wildlife habitats available. The sheer volume of visitors means that, however carefully people keep to codes of appropriate behaviour, they inevitably destroy the thing they have come to enjoy. The paradox of destructive tourism continues.

Local populations, many of whom derive little benefit from the influx, are adversely affected. Whether in low-paid service employment in commercial enterprises dependent on tourism or in the traditional industries of the area, locals cannot compete with the spending power of metropolitan outsiders. As in other national parks the Lake District has real problems in providing adequate affordable housing for its resident population. With over 350,000 second homes nationally, the competition for the few properties on the market is intense. Demand from holiday visitors and those seeking to retire in a well loved landscape (the permanent tourists) serve to deny access to housing to succeeding generations of local villagers. Young people of the district are forced out not only by the shortage of well paid employment, but also by the impossibility of finding affordable permanent accommodation.

The balance sheet reveals the divisive impact of tourism on an area like the Lake District. The problem is a continuing one, since each year sees an ever-growing number of visitors, and the negative balance threatens to destroy the very landscape that attracts the tourists. The calls for protection and conservation become even more desperate, and the impact of many of the proposed 'solutions' appears increasingly draconian. Park authorities worry about balancing access with a suitable 'carrying capacity' of a vulnerable environment. Controls through car-parking limits, building restrictions and vehicle cordons appear ever more likely if the much loved landscapes are indeed to be preserved for future mass enjoyment.

Questions and exercises

1 Do you consider that the disadvantages of tourism to an area like the Lake District outweigh its benefits?
2 Should national parks attempt to cater for a range of tastes by encouraging 'honeypot' concentrations and thereby leaving other areas less developed and congested?
3 Do you think it feasible to introduce further restrictions on the use of cars in an effort to reduce congestion and pollution?

Further reading

The problems of conserving the national parks while enabling access for growing numbers of visitors are addressed in 'National Parks Today', the quarterly newspaper of the Countryside Commission and the park authorities, in addition to the texts discussed in Chapter 3.

'Coping with change': football league clubs under pressure

Association football developed in earnest in Britain in the last quarter of the nineteenth century, and much of the investment in the physical infrastructure of the game occurred then, and subsequently before the First World War. Between 1889 and 1910 fifty-eight of the current major professional clubs moved into grounds they developed on the edge of the then built-up area of conurbations (Inglis,1987).

Clubs bought fields to develop in competition with speculative builders and thus pre-empted the spread of terraced housing in at least one section of the densely built working class suburbs. Near to local populations and served by trams and omnibuses, the grounds developed the characteristic appearance of concrete terracing, spectator rails, open 'kops', girder-work and giant shed roofs. Spartan spectator facilities for Edwardian working class males and no concessions to anything other than pedestrian or public transport access were the order of the day. Clubs were developed historically, and these traditional settings were central to fan loyalty and spectator support. Playing success, not comfortable or salubrious settings, was the basis for enduring affection for 'home' grounds. An intense territoriality and an emotional investment in a historic setting have always been central to the mass spectator experience.

By the late twentieth century soccer presented a very different picture of decline and physical underinvestment. An increasingly affluent, mobile and volatile population demonstrated declining support for the professional game. Total attendances at Football League matches in England and Wales declined from a post-war peak of over 41 million in 1948–49, to 20 million in 1981–82, and stabilized around 19 million by 1990–1, as competition from alternative pastimes and a dissatisfaction with the 'product' manifested themselves (see Table 4.2).

There are many theories behind the loss of paying spectators. Some blame hooliganism and fears for safety, others the defensive displays on offer, or the greater selectivity of a more discerning affluent market, with many more diverting options available. Whatever the cause, the reality is frequently that of historic clubs often technically bankrupt and necessarily subsidized as an indulgence of wealthy directors. These historic sporting organizations, located in outmoded stadia on often quite valuable urban sites, present a context ready for change.

Table 4.2 Fluctuating attendances at English First Division/ Premier League games

Years	Average attendance
1961–62	26,106
1966–67	30,829
1971–72	31,352
1976–77	29,540
1981–82	22,556
1986–87	19,800
1991–92	21,622
1992–93	21,125 (Premier League)

Source: *Social Trends*, 1994

Soccer has not been uniquely affected. Other professional sports are equally pressured. Greyhound racing declined from a post-war peak of seventy-seven officially registered tracks to sixty-four locations by May 1961, when betting shops were legalized, and currently has only thirty-seven licensed tracks. Famous and marketable assets, such as Harringay, became developed as a Sainsbury superstore.

The professional sport of Rugby League reflected similar economic circumstances. One of the first 'victims' was Hunslet RLFC, which was a founder member of the League in 1895 and whose Parkside Grounds in Inner Leeds (opened for football and cricket in 1888 and hence representing a particularly extensive and valuable real estate asset for an unsuccessful Second Division club), were sold for warehouse development in 1973 for £300,000. Other clubs have also capitalized on the sale of 'spare' training pitches and parts of car parks (Wigan RLFC's sold for a reported £2.5 million) and even entire grounds. Both York RLFC which sold its Clarence Street ground in 1988 for £700,000, and Hull Kingston Rovers, selling Craven Park for £4 million have seen the advantage of a new purpose-built stadium at the edge of town (Spink, 1989b).

Soccer clubs have not found it as easy to follow in the footsteps of these clubs or even Football League rivals like Scunthorpe and Walsall. The Taylor Report recommendations into crowd safety in the wake of the Hillsborough disaster of April 1989 severely restricted ground capacity and ordered all-seater stadia for Premier League and First Division clubs. Faced with necessary capital investment and reduced spectator numbers many clubs have considered redevelopment or relocation. A Royal Town Planning Institute survey of all ninety-two English League clubs in 1990 found twenty-three clubs considering commercial development of part of their grounds, and there were forty-two proposals for entire relocation being investigated (Shepley, 1990).

For many grounds retail development was the most lucrative and most favoured option, with housing, hotels and offices as alternative possibilities. In many cases the only problem was that of the original location, giving poor accessibility, and limited by the constraints imposed by nearby housing. The very reason why clubs wished to move from cramped stadia was often the basis for local-authority opposition to a commercial redevelopment of their sites.

Another problem has been that of finding a suitable extensive cheap site for the relocation of ground, training areas and spectator car parking. Public concern over traffic congestion, possible hooliganism, and the threat to green-belt areas have halted the possible suburbanization of several clubs.

Oxford United, whose Manor Ground is set in the residential district of Headington with no room for
expansion, has attempted several times in the 1990s
to find an environmentally and politically acceptable
green-field site on the edge of the city. Southampton
FC, with the Dell limited in capacity to around 14,000
by the demands for an all-seater stadium, has seen
the advantages of exploring possible relocation.

Sunderland Football Club has been desperate to build
a new stadium before the impact of the Taylor Report
compelling all-seater Premier League and First
Division grounds by the start of the 1994–5 season
reduces Roker Park's capacity from 29,000 to 9000.
In Sunderland, as elsewhere, the search for a new site
has generated opposition, with the powerful local
Nissan car producer objecting to a football ground as
a potential neighbour for its plant, mainly through
concern over road congestion affecting component
delivery.

Some clubs have capitalized on their grounds and
decamped, like Bristol Rovers and Millwall. St
Johnstone in the Scottish League sold their site in
central Perth to a supermarket chain for redevelopment and moved to a brand new all-seated stadium
for 10,000 spectators on the edge of town. Others, like
Huddersfield Town, have been prepared to leave the
Leeds Road ground after 84 years for the prospect of a
purpose-built municipal stadium shared with the
local Rugby League side.

The scale of investment in such schemes requires
considerable capital backing, which falling gates
rarely underwrite. Most moves are backed by wealthy
directors or owners, or follow the example of conti-
nental Europe in leasing a share of a municipally
owned stadium. With that level of subsidy, impressive
venues of the scale of the San Siro or Nimes can be
achieved. For most struggling British clubs and their
long suffering supporters those prospects are as dis-

tant as actually playing Inter or AC Milan. The majority struggle on with the residual capital of the Edwardian era.

Questions and exercises

1 Do you know of any local clubs intending to relocate or redevelop parts of their ground in an effort to raise capital? What has been the extent of opposition to such proposals?
2 How important do you consider the atmosphere of the older grounds for the enjoyment of current supporters? Will redevelopment and all-seater stadia discourage traditional support?
3 Will new facilities encourage a wider section of the population to attend matches or will they simply destroy the old territoriality?
4 To what extent can out-of-town grounds solve problems of congestion and hooliganism?

Further reading

The context of professional soccer as a leisure-time activity has been well explored in texts like Nicholas Fishwick (1989) *English Football and Society, 1910–1950*, and Stephen Wagg (1984) *The Football World*. For a thorough examination of the stadia themselves, Simon Inglis (1987) *The Football Grounds of Great Britain*, and John Bale (1993) *Sport, Space and the City*, provide comprehensive and impressive accounts. For a more atmospheric account of the realities of being a supporter Nick Hornby (1992) *Fever Pitch*, provides an insider's viewpoint, which is superbly reinforced for Rugby League, by Ian Clayton and Michael Steele (1993) *When Push Comes to Shove*.

'Going for broke': leisure developments and city image

Another feature of postmodern change in leisure and society is the way in which local authorities have increasingly felt the need to market their area in a competitive arena of bidding for limited international investment capital. David Harvey has detailed this transformation of governance from the managerialism of welfarist economies of the 1960s to the active entrepreneurship of the 1980s and 1990s (Harvey, 1989). He has commented on a 'serial investment' in spectacle, special events and new civic investment as city after city refurbished its historic industrial quarters, its waterfront or riverside, and staged everything from garden festivals, bicycle or power-boat races to rallies of tall ships or vintage cars. In every case the elements of fun, carnival and a positive leisure image are seen as working to give a good impression of the quality of life and environment available in that municipality.

London Docklands probably epitomizes all the elements of such a transformation, with the added advantage to the transmission of its image of a metropolitan location and the support of a committed government to a 'flagship project'. Here the objective was the regeneration of a large area of mainly derelict former dockland in a prime location east of the City of London.

The task was not to be entrusted to the local authorities of the area but to the first of the government-appointed urban development quangos in the establishment of the London Docklands Development Corporation in 1981. The aim was the creation of a much more integrated urban structure, linking employment, housing, retail and leisure facilities, to overcome the disadvantages of the nineteenth century functionally segregated city, and also to reverse the local consequences of economic decline and neglect.

Despite the investment of vast amounts in public funds and the creation of 20,000 jobs, the whole concept was overtaken by the deepening recession of the late 1980s. The problems were crystallized and symbolized in the Canary Wharf Tower as its developers Olympia and York went bankrupt.

The success of London Docklands was very much tied to the success of commercial property development and so suffered directly from general economic set-backs hitting the South East. Its initial high profile and the presence of the mass media nearby has served to emphasise its problems and mistakes. Nevertheless the transformation of large areas has been achieved and the imagery of a waterside diversity of postmodern architectural styles has had considerable and lasting impact on the strategies adopted for other places.

Another example of image change in the 1980s incorporating leisure and cultural forms was the campaign to rehabilitate Glasgow. Hit by the monetarist spending cuts and economic recession in the early years of the decade, Glasgow's traditional industries of engineering, dockwork and shipbuilding declined rapidly (Donnison and Middleton, 1987).

Glasgow's civic leaders and business people saw the need to reverse decline, and recognized the importance of city imagery and place marketing in postmodern Britain. Their campaign through the 1980s, although linked to less grandiose physical redevelopment than in London Docklands, focused on the broadly negative image of the city perceived by outsiders. This image was considered to present a historic obstacle to contemporary capital development. Their target was the traditional British stereotype of the city as a tough, brawling, lawless, left-wing militant, unionized bastion of organized labour, pervaded by the ethos of 'hard' men with their pints of 'heavy' and a propensity for violence, public and domestic, particularly on a Saturday night in Sauchiehall Street, the Gorbals or Govan. The campaign was to tackle that image of the city and to replace it.

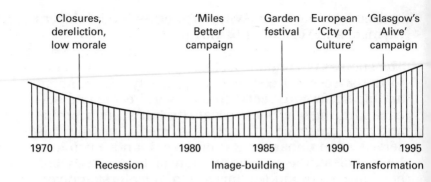

Figure 4.2 Timescale of Glasgow's transformation

The first stage, in 1983, was that of a more localized and Scottish-based campaign to improve the image for inhabitants and frequent visitors, using the 'Glasgow's Miles Better' slogan. Working to boost civic pride locally became the starting point for wider publicity, using hallmark events like the Garden Festival of 1988 to disseminate knowledge of the historic architecture of Charles Rennie Mackintosh and the prestigious art collections of the Burrell and other galleries.

The cultural focus for tourism and image rehabilitation was repaid as city visitors increased from 700,000 in 1982 to over 2 million by 1987 (Davidson,1992), and Glasgow was selected as European 'City of Culture' in 1990. During that year attendances at cultural events and attactions amounted to 6.5 million and generated an estimated net income of £10–14 million for the city and created 5,500 jobs for the year. As Figure 4.2 shows, the significance of leisure and cultural forms in transforming the city's image was considerable and parallels the more general promotion of other old industrial cities elsewhere as suitable places in which to visit, tour, invest and even, live.

Many provincial cities have followed the leads of

London Docklands and of Glasgow. Another with a heavy-industrial heritage facing economic decline was Sheffield. Here the strategy to change 'Steel City' has incorporated both sports and cultural investment.

Facing similar negative image problems in the perceptions of outside decision-makers, the Labour-controlled City Council sought to improve Sheffield's image by attracting what might be seen as a prestigious sporting event as a 'mega-event' or 'hallmark' event to encourage media attention. Such attempts bear witness to the place of spectacle in successful postmodern place-marketing.

The city bid for, and was awarded, the 1991 World Student Games. To host the athletics, swimming and other sports required considerable investment in facilities and the replacement of a number of ageing sports venues in the city. Such a strategy was inevitably high-risk, expensive, and not as prestigious as staging an event like the Olympic Games, but was backed by the City Council. Part of its enthusiasm was based upon over-optimistic forecasts of possible revenue and development costs, along with hopes of greater governmental support, if not even of a complete change of central government to a more supportive regime.

The World Student Games became a key element of the image-building investment supported by local politicians. Various large recreation complexes, like Ponds Forge for swimming, Don Valley Stadium for athletics and the Hillsborough Arena for indoor competition were constructed. The Games went ahead successfully and generated the usual amount of publicity for a sub-Olympic and international student event.

This aspect of the city transformation strategy, given the costs and returns, was inevitably quite high-risk. Some of the investment still generates positive publicity, as Ponds Forge subsequently became a European Championship swimming venue, and the other facilities are used for national and international competitions and events. The cost to the Sheffield local taxpayers was large (an event debt of around £10 million and 20-year capital debts of over £400 million) and the final evaluation, given that the facilities worth over £150 million are still generating publicity and available for local use, depends finally upon political commitment as much as any readily objective cost-benefit analysis (Roche, 1994).

The other strand in Sheffield's campaign has centred on the promotion of cultural industries as part of economic regeneration and city-image projection. Following the direction set by the Greater London Council's cultural strategy, the city has attempted to develop local talents in musical performance and recording by establishing the Red Tape Studios. Here multi-media production skills can be linked to the education of local people in what is perceived as a viable successor to the heavy industry of the past. The development of the city's Cultural Industries Quarter, in association with the Crucible Theatre, local orchestras, pop groups and performance artists, the Red Tape Studios, Leadmill Centre and other city venues, is seen as boosting not only employment prospects but contributing positively towards economic regeneration through tourism and positive publicity.

Such has been the competition for a declining share of 'foot-loose' investment capital in the 1980s and 1990s, that most local authorities have developed a strategy for image-building and economic development centred on leisure, culture and tourism. Few have made the extensive physical investment of London Docklands or even Sheffield's sporting facilities, but the drive to exploit heritage, local crafts and skills in a celebration of locational diversity and uniqueness has, paradoxically, followed a similar pattern.

The image chosen for transmission is frequently highly selective and sanitized, and is often revealing as to what it omits, e.g. the importance of the slave trade in Bristol and Liverpool's past, as much as what it includes. It often focuses on high art as an elite form of internationally valued civic currency and tends to neglect working-class history and mundane architecture rather than the prestigious civic façade. However, in all their efforts cities show the significance of leisure, culture, and recreational environments in their promotion of place, and demonstrate the importance of these in the lifestyles of both locals and visitors.

Questions and exercises

1 How has your local city attempted to improve its image or sell its advantages? Which features have been used to market the place, and have they included leisure activities or mega-events?
2 Are the bids for world athletic or other sporting or cultural events worthwhile? Do you think the advantages of hosting the Olympic Games or the Commonwealth Games outweigh the costs for British cities?
3 Do you consider that the city images developed have been highly selective? Which elements of historic heritage have been emphasized and which neglected in a town or city with which you are familiar?
4 How much do you think cultural industries and the promotion of arts and cultural quarters can contribute to the economic regeneration of post-industrial cities?

Further reading

The nature of contemporary tourism is explored in John Urry (1990) *The Tourist Gaze*, and the role of tourism in city marketing and image-building is usefully detailed in Christopher Law (1993) *Urban Tourism*. The contribution of cultural industries is advocated by Franco Bianchini, M Fisher, J Montgomery, and K Walpole (1988) *City Centre Culture: The Role of the Arts in the Revitalization of Towns and Cities*, and in Franco Bianchini and Michael Parkinson (1993) *Cultural Policy and Urban Regeneration.*

Conclusion

Leisure and the environment integrates participants and activities within the context as an essential part of the experience. This exploration of leisure environments has necessarily reflected the diversity of people, pastimes and venues involved. By its centrality to existence, leisure encompasses all facets of economic, social, cultural and political life and so is inherent in the processes of change operating in society, and any study of leisure in context is inevitably as diverse as that society.

Forecasting the future in leisure is thus as exacting as in any other facet of life. Whether one utilizes trend extrapolation or tries to make inspired guesses along Delphic lines, the future, like the past, is a 'distant country', and difficult to discern.

Currently, leisure participants, the people in the equation, seem as disparate and polarized as ever. Chapter 1 examined the aspects of poverty and social attitude that disadvantage substantial minorities in society. The gaps in economic resources and the shortage of 'cultural capital' to appreciate and participate in the full range of recreational opportunities has clearly not diminished in the last 20 years. Indeed, not only the free time of the poor is threatened as economic pressures of long hours, dual roles, stress, increased productivity, job insecurity and unpaid overtime, consume potential leisure for even the more affluent and socially successful.

It is the poor, however, who highlight the crucial interconnections between people's leisure activities and issues of access and accessibility. The poverty, outlined earlier, restricts and constrains through limits on spending power necessary for participation in so many contemporary activities. Physically, accessibility and mobility are just as significant constraints as finance upon participation in increasingly dispersed and decentralized activities, for which available transport facilities are vitally necessary.

Changing transport policy, with an emphasis on possession of private cars and reduction in direct subsidy to all forms of public transport, exacerbates the problems for those constrained through income, age or disability. Increasing privatization, whether of road or rail, has contributed to greater reliance on the market and less public intervention and regulation, with socially divisive consequences. Transport provision increasingly needs to be considered as a regressive element in leisure accessibility. Only those users able to bear the escalating expense can avail themselves of deteriorating public services, while electoral pressure frequently seems to be exerted towards assistance for private motorists and the road construction lobby.

The negative consequences of a private car focus for transport policy are publicly apparent in the conflicts over road building threats to historic rural landscapes. Less publicized is the long-term damage visited upon inner urban communities by the imposition of divisive, dangerous and polluting major highways which with each subsequent 'improvement' consume vast areas of homes, employment and open space, in a vain attempt to cope with spiralling volumes of suburban car use. Public action to cope with ever increasing transport demands and expectations and the scale of potential and actual damage and social division has thus become one of the key issues affecting the environment and consequently leisure activities into the next millennium.

Activities have always risen and fallen in popularity as changing generations innovate, discard or re-discover leisure forms of the past. The nature of leisure changes according to the time, resources, expectations and aspirations of each age, and postmodern society has encouraged increased individual and domestic entertainment to reverse the collective trends of previous modern eras.

These changes have their impact on leisure spaces, as this volume has recorded. The dynamics of urban and rural land use ensure that continuing conflict and competition seem inevitable. Increasing commercialism and a recently diminishing role for the public sector in provision make profitability an increasingly significant driving force of change. Whether the market leads to Schumpeter's 'creative destruction' in its operation or simply anarchic over-provision flooding areas of effective demand, remains to be seen. Paradoxically, occuring at a time of growing concern over sustainability and resource depletion, this kind of thoughtless and unplanned exploitation seems less and less affordable for an acquisitive globalized society.

Changing patterns of popularity and profitability mean that leisure spaces rise and fall with styles, fashions and economic cycles, within the workings of commercial and political pressures. The nature of contemporary urban life ensures that leisure or free time activities remain a public concern from social order if not from social welfare considerations. Continued intervention, however residual, seems likely, and ensures that a matrix of provision, perhaps of minimal standard, is distributed quite generally. However, issues of the private domain seem to dominate as we approach the next millennium.

At present, as this volume has shown, there seems little that is leisured about contemporary rural and particularly urban settings. However, whether these are national parks, canal-side walks, sports stadia or shopping malls, they remain significant as the venues for our enjoyable experiences in leisure and recreation, and represent an essential aspect of study as the places where we choose to spend our free time.

Bibliography

Bale, J (1993) *Sport, Space and the City*, Routledge,London.

Bianchini, F, Fisher M, Montgomery, J and Walpole K (1988) *City Centre Culture: The Role of the Arts in the Revitalization of Towns and Cities*, Centre for Local Economic Strategies, Manchester.

Bianchini, F and Parkinson, M (1993) *Cultural Policy and Urban Regeneration*, Manchester University Press, Manchester.

Blunden, J and Curry, N (1988) *A Future for Our Countryside*, Basil Blackwell, Oxford.

Central Statistical Office (1994) *Social Trends*, HMSO, London.

Countryside Commission (1991) *Caring for the Countryside*, CCP 351, Countryside Commission, Manchester.

Countryside Commission (1992) *Enjoying the Countryside: Policies for People*, CCP 371, Countryside Commission, Manchester.

Countryside Commission,(1993) *Countryside*, May–June, No 61.

Clarke, J and Critcher, C (1985) *The Devil Makes Work*, Macmillan, London.

Clayton, I and Steele, M (1993) *When Push Comes to Shove*, Yorkshire Arts Circus, Castleford, West Yorkshire.

Davidson, R (1992) *Tourism in Europe*, Pitman, London.

Deem, R (1986) *All Work and No Play?*, Open University Press, Milton Keynes.

Donnison, D and Middleton, A (1987) *Regenerating the inner city; Glasgow's Experience*, Routledge and Kegan Paul, London.

Elson, J (1986) *Green Belts*, Butterworth-Heinemann, Oxford.

English Tourist Board (1992) Annual Report, ETB, London.

Featherstone, M (1991) *Consumer Culture and Postmodernism*, Sage Publications, London.

Fishwick, N (1989) *English Football and Society, 1910–1950*, Manchester University Press, Manchester.

Gardner, C and Sheppard, J (1989) *Consuming Passion*, Unwin Hyman, London.

Glyptis, S (1989) *Leisure and Unemployment*, Open University Press, Milton Keynes.

Glyptis, S (1991) *Countryside Recreation*, Longman, London.

Greed, C (1993) *Introducing Town Planning*, Longman, London.

Harrison, C (1991) *Countryside Recreation in a Changing Society*, The TMS Partnership, London.

Harvey, D (1989) *The Condition of Postmodernity*, Basil Blackwell, Oxford.

Haywood, L, Kew, F, Bramham P, Spink, J, Capenerhurst, J and Henry I (1989) *Understanding Leisure*, Hutchinson, London.

Henry I and Spink J,(1990) 'Social Theory, Planning and Management,' Chapter 7, in Henry I,(ed.) *Management and Planning in the Leisure Industries*, Macmillan, London.

Henry, I (1993) *The Politics of Leisure Policy*, Macmillan, London.

Hornby, N (1992) *Fever Pitch*, Victor Gollancz, London.

Inglis, S (1987) *The Football Grounds of Great Britain*, Willow, London.

King, A and Clifford, S (1987) *Holding Your Ground*, Wildwood House, Aldershot.

Kivell, P (1993) *Land and the City*, Routledge, London.

Knox, P (1987) *Urban Social Geography*, Longman Group, Harlow.

Law, C (1993) *Urban Tourism*, Mansell, London

Little, J Peake, L and Richardson, P (1988) *Women in Cities: Gender and the Urban Environment*, Macmillan, Basingstoke.

North Yorkshire County Council (1979) *County Structure Plan; Written Statement*, NYCC, Northallerton.

Roche, M (1994) 'Mega-Events and Urban Policy', *Annals of Tourism Research*, vol. 21, No. 1, pp. 1–19.

Shepley, C (1990) 'Planning and Football League Grounds,'*The Planner*, 28 September, pp. 15–17.

Shoard, M (1987) *This Land is Our Land*, Paladin Grafton, London.

Spink, J (1989a) 'Urban Development, Leisure Facilities and the Inner City,' in Bramham P, Henry I, Mommaas H, and van der Poel H, *Leisure and Urban Processes*, Routledge, London.

Spink, J (1989b) 'Losing Ground; Development Pressures and Recreation Spaces', *Newsletter*, July, Leisure Studies Association.

Urry, J (1990) *The Tourist Gaze*, Sage Publications, London

Wagg, S (1984) *The Football World*, Harvester, Brighton.

Walvin, J (1978) *Leisure and Society: 1830–1950*, Longman, London.

Williams, R (1973) *The Country and the City*, Chatto and Windus, London.

Index

Quarrying, 55, 59–60, 73, 89

Racial minorities, 11–13, 16–18, 33, 56
Racism, 13, 17
Rambling, 4, 63, 66
Reformism, 25
Resorts, 2, 5
Retailing, 23, 33–6, 39, 42–3, 46, 76–82, 101
Rugby league, 100–1
Rural areas, 55–75

Second homes, 71–3, 89, 97
Set-aside, 87–92
Sexism, 13–14
Sheffield, 78, 104–6
Shopping, 4, 23, 31, 33–5, 39–42, 76–81
Sites of Special Scientific Interest, 64
Social closure, 17
Sociology, 5, 11
Spectator sport, 9–10, 37, 41–3, 98–103
Sports halls, 5, 23–4
Suburbs, 32, 49–50, 52, 71
Swimming pools, 35, 37, 43–6, 52, 105

Team sports, 43
Television, 4, 7–8, 10
Thatcherism, 25
Theatre, 9, 23, 34, 37, 41, 43, 48
Tourism, 31, 40, 60, 63, 73, 89, 92–8, 103, 106
Tourists, 3, 55
Trespass, 66–7

Unemployed, 11, 13, 19–20, 24, 27, 33
Urban areas, 3–5, 17–18, 28–54
Urban fringe, 32, 35, 69, 74

Video (recording), 4, 8, 36–7, 41–2, 80

Waterfronts, 39–41, 101
Wildlife and Countryside Act 1981, 63–4, 69
Williams, R., 65
Women, 11–15, 18, 22, 27, 34, 77, 91
Work, 22–3, 39–40, 42

Yorkshire Dales, 89–91
Youth, 16, 19–20, 24